Leone Magiera

PAVAROTTI
UP CLOSE

RICORDI

Original title: *Pavarotti visto da vicino*.

Translation by Sophie Martin. Translation of the Technical Appendixes by Anna Herklotz.

Cover photographs: Judith Kovacs, Publifoto, Roncaglia
Back cover photograph: Fabio Fantuzzi
Cover design: Giuseppe Spada

NR 140048
ISBN 978-88-7592- 782-0

CONTENTS

PREFACE

After Luciano Pavarotti's death on 6th September 2007, I decided to complete my story of his life by giving an account of the twenty-three years between 1985 and 2007, when we worked together constantly with only an occasional and very brief intermission. The second part of this book begins where my first book left off – his tour of China.

I have recounted the most important stages of his astounding career during those years, relying solely on my memory. I wrote it in a single draft, carried along on a wave of emotion that swept over me at his death. I hope the reader will forgive me if the precise dates of certain events are missing, or if the occasional detail is not totally accurate.

My aim is not to write a scholarly work but to reconstruct the events I felt to be most important, exactly as I remember them, from my personal experience of that fantastic character, Luciano.

I decided to retain and extend the technical analyses contained in the first edition, given the interest they had aroused in students of singing from various parts of the world. These appendices, gathered at the end of the book, constitute a brief but practical treatise on singing, which even non-specialist lovers of opera will find accessible.

The efficacy of these short "lessons" is not, I believe, entirely due to their technical content. Drawing from first hand knowledge of Pavarotti's vocal and artistic development, I have tried to show that besides purely vocal talent – a gift of God that Luciano often talked of – other qualities are needed: equal measures of humility and confidence in one's own abilities, experience of studying and of life, lucky artistic encounters and the capacity for close and profound observation of the ever-changing world of music. A combination of these elements is to be found in all great artists' lives; they are essential for building a successful career, although few can aspire to repeating the artistic journey of the man whom I consider to be the greatest tenor of the century.

Leone Magiera

PREFACE TO THE FIRST EDITION
by Gianandrea Gavazzeni

There are two fundamental reasons why this book on the career of Luciano Pavarotti (dealing with the studies and success, the art and the legend) is different from other works about famous singers, either still performing or part of musical history.

First, it is written by a multi-disciplinary musician who has worked regularly over years for such organisations as La Scala in Milan, the Teatro Comunale in Bologna and its counterpart in Florence; an operatic singing director of vast expertise and wisdom, a lieder accompanist of great delicacy and skill whose concert credits run from the German Romantics to Mahler and the Impressionists; and a conductor who has worked extremely closely with Pavarotti himself. It is these qualities, this stature, that mark off Magiera from the authors of other biographies, which rarely rise above a mixture of chronology and hagiography.

Magiera's language alone would justify this claim: it is exact in its terminology and its technical correlations. Herein lies the essential difference from other works of this kind: Magiera alternates and accompanies the story of Pavarotti's life with a musical commentary – paying specific attention to vocal technique – in relation to the character of the man. These observations, both theoretical and practical, are expressed with great clarity, and allow the text to be read on two levels: one as a treatise for musicians, the other as a fascinating story for the music lover who knows enough to appreciate the challenges of a singer's life and their connection with facts.

The originality – one might even say the novelty – of Magiera's approach consists in precisely this: the alternation of the life story of an artist with a technical and didactic commentary that sheds light on particular issues and through them on problems of a more general nature. There is no place here for hagiography; this is a serious work, filled with valuable insights and personal testimony of the life and development of an opera singer and musician.

In addition, Pavarotti's early formative experiences as a singer are recounted in precise and specific terms, without the approximations that are sometimes – or often – used in such cases. The fact that both author and subject are from Modena, an ancient province with a rich, robust and living culture, adds further authenticity to the telling.

Magiera's account of Pavarotti's early vocal and musical career is particularly sensitive to this cultural context, and is underwritten by the long years of friendship and artistic collaboration between the two men. We are given the whole story of this initial phase, the first attempts, the studies, the first steps in making a career, the struggles with technique – that perennial problem faced by all conscientious singers who are capable of reflection on themselves and on the psychological and physiological realities of their craft. All of this is described here truthfully, without rhetoric or pomposity. Due space is given to his period of study with Ettore Campogalliani, another legend in his own right, a man of Mantova – a city which we both love...

This is, in sum, a book for two voices: protagonist and companion, biographer and musical analyst, in close harmony. It is an exceptionally well-judged and illuminating piece of work.

AUTHOR BIOGRAPHICAL NOTES

Conductor, pianist, discoverer of new singing talent, Leone Magiera has accompanied the musical careers of stars such as Mirella Freni, Ruggero Raimondi, Luciano Pavarotti and Carmela Remigio.

Born in Modena, Magiera became a pianist at an early age, going on to study piano with Lino Rastelli, Giorgio Vidusso and Alberto Mozzati. His versatile musical talent soon led him to the conductor's podium of the most prestigious orchestras and opera houses in the world, and to long-term collaboration with conductors such as Claudio Abbado, Carlo Maria Giulini, Herbert von Karajan and Carlos Kleiber. He has been chorus master in Bologna, Genova and at La Scala in Milan, and has accompanied all the greatest singers on the international scene in recitals throughout his career.

He accompanied Luciano Pavarotti in over a thousand appearances in theatres and arenas the world over.

He has been an artistic director of La Scala and of Maggio Musicale Fiorentino. He has also had an intensive career as a singing teacher: at the Conservatorio in Bologna, at Glyndebourne and Salzburg festivals. He has written numerous books on singing, published by Ricordi; they have been translated into several languages.

A long and wide-ranging list of recordings with the most prestigious international labels bears witness to his many-sided talent, both as soloist and conductor.

Leone Magiera's website is www.leonemagiera.it and his e-mail address is info@leonemagiera.it

INTRODUCTION

I showed the proofs of this work to a close friend and colleague who teaches singing at the Conservatorio. He gave me his professional opinion, which was that for a "treatise on singing" it was insufficiently thorough. "You make no reference to the crico-arytenoid and thyro-arytenoid muscles," he said disapprovingly; "nor to the mystery of the false vocal cords or Morgagni's ventricle."

Another friend, who has a more or less permanent seat in the gods at the Teatro Regio in Parma, took a different view: "For a biography, it doesn't tell us enough about the hero's love life or his hobbies".

I tried to explain to my colleague that the libraries of musical academies are filled with books on singing which devote hundreds of pages to the most detailed descriptions of the vocal apparatus, and I did not think it worth my while simply adding to their number. I told my opera-loving friend that Pavarotti's private life, his passion for football and horses, had been more than adequately treated in the gossip pages of newspapers and magazines, and I could see no purpose in going over this familiar material yet again. Neither of them seemed convinced by my explanations.

Some of my students were more enthusiastic.

"At last!" said Katya. "A treatise on singing that really goes to the heart of the problems of technique and artistic expression instead of rambling on about someone or other's ventricle..."

"Morgagni's?" I suggested.

" – exactly; or the thyro-something muscles. I'm sorry, Professor, it's the thyro-..."

"Thyro-arytenoid," I said, wishing to save this voluble ash-blonde Swedish mezzo-soprano from further embarrassment.

Then there was Francesca, an old friend of the family who worked closely with Adua, Pavarotti's first wife. She was surprised to read in a "biography" about episodes in Luciano's life of which even his wife and children were unaware.

Naturally enough, I began to ask myself whether I had in fact written a "biography" or a "treatise on singing". From this small survey of readers' reactions it appeared that the two elements were indissolubly fused. This was not my original intention.

In recounting my lifelong friendship with Pavarotti, I had clearly found it impossible to separate my personal recollections of his life from a description of his highly idiosyncratic and original methods of study, which brought such splendid and well-known results.

I would add that as a professional who has spent many years grappling with the problems of singing and interpretation, I believe it is essential, for an understanding of Pavarotti's development, to focus on the very close relationship between his native gifts, his method of study, his life choices and the artistic flowering of his maturity.

PART ONE

A TALENT DISCOVERED

Luciano Pavarotti had the great good fortune to grow up in a home where music was played.

His father Fernando, a baker by necessity rather than choice, had the voice and spirit of an artist, but lacked one of the most important qualities of a singer: confidence. His stage fright would begin as soon as he faced an audience: an icy sweat would break out on his forehead, his throat would tighten and his legs would feel weak.

Not surprisingly, his considerable vocal talents were diminished by this nervous condition and his hopes of a career as a soloist soon came to nothing.

Fernando's great passion for singing, though painfully inhibited in public, was freely indulged at home. One can imagine little Luciano, wide-eyed with admiration, listening to his father's intense, unaccompanied renderings of "Spirto gentil", "Che gelida manina", "Ch'ella mi creda", and "Nessun dorma"…

As a boy in Modena, Luciano joined his father as a member of the Società Corale Gioachino Rossini, a group of music-lovers and fans of *bel canto* who would use a stopwatch to measure the length of a high note or a *filatura*, then hotly discuss the results as if they were comparing sprinters on a sports field.

These were Modena's golden years of opera. The Teatro Comunale, a 19th century architectural gem, had recently re-opened after the War, and offered audiences the chance to hear the best voices of the time.

Carlo Alberto Cappelli, a highly cultured private impresario, toured artists of the calibre of Magda Olivero, Mario Del Monaco, Ferruccio Tagliavini, Giulietta Simionato, and Mario Filippeschi, as well as young talents such as Giuseppe Di Stefano, Renata Tebaldi, Franco Corelli and Giuseppe Taddei.

At the Corale Rossini these performances were subjected to minutely detailed and usually unforgiving critiques. The criticism was of course wasted on such singers, who are now justifiably considered to be sacred figures.

Olivero was accused of having a voice with a tight, displeasing quiver "like a mandolin"; Simionato, as Carmen, was charged with "sluttish vulgarity"(!); Del Monaco's voice was not considered dark enough for the role of Otello. No one escaped criticism. Young Luciano followed these discussions closely, but did not share their burning fanaticism. In fact, his admiration for the great performers increased daily, as did his love of music and singing generally.

One day Modena hosted two great celebrities: Lina Pagliughi and Beniamino Gigli, who were starring in *Lucia di Lammermoor*. They were both somewhat advanced in years, and perhaps not at the height of their powers. Although the performance was a great success, the local critics were cruel when they met afterwards. They censured Gigli for his sobs and affectations, Pagliughi for a lack of warmth in her expression; and the two singers' stage presence was judged to be ridiculous because of their excessive size.

On that occasion Luciano, a mature-looking twelve-year-old, boldly defended the great tenor from the Marche, even though he was aware that the man was in poor physical shape. The following day he endured a long wait for the honour of meeting him and shaking his hand.

Gigli was doing vocal exercises in a small room at the Teatro Comunale. Although he was approaching sixty, he practised every day without fail. Luciano waited patiently. When he finally saw Gigli emerge, he suddenly felt intimidated by the presence of the great man. He could think of nothing better to say than: "Maestro, how many years have you been studying?"

Gigli replied, in a kindly tone: "Until five minutes ago, my boy."

This was the only time Gigli and Pavarotti met, and their conversation ended there, yet Gigli's concise wisdom gave the young Luciano much to think about.

Some years later, at one of the Corale Rossini's social evenings, Pavarotti's voice attracted the attention of his fellow members. They were holding a celebration dinner for the anniversary of the society, an occasion which would have horrified today's advocates of a low-fat diet. For several hours the gallant singers had been doing battle with steaming dishes of tortellini, lasagne, tagliatelle, chickens, pigs' trotters and much else besides. Rivers of sparkling red Lambrusco flowed, further inflaming the heated discussions between the supporters of Miguel Fleta and Beniamino Gigli. One of the older members was claiming that Tamagno's Otello was the best he had ever heard, and his nostalgic and exaggerated reminiscences were starting to annoy the young supporters of an up-and-coming tenor, Mario Del Monaco. The appearance at the table of an enormous round of Parmesan cheese, the staple diet of these descendants of Alessandro Tassoni, served to temper the controversy just a little.

People began to sense a buzz in the atmosphere as the moment approached for the best voices in the choir to compete, late into the night, in a battle of romantic songs and epic high notes. Friends had already begun coaxing Fernando – unanimously considered to have the best voice as well as the best appetite in the choir – to overcome his nerves and sing his *pièce de résistance*, "Nessun dorma". After much insistence, Fernando agreed.

He was not entirely free from nerves, but the fact that he was among friends, in a festive and convivial atmosphere, reassured him greatly.

At around four in the morning Fernando's B natural rang out, in Calaf's famous phrase, "All'alba vincerò", with a beauty and firmness of tone reminiscent of the voice of Galliano Masini. Everyone broke into spontaneous applause. Fernando thanked them, obviously very moved, and then, almost ashamed of what he was about to say, mumbled softly and barely intelligibly: "But my son Luciano can also hit that note."

These words did not go unnoticed, and the teenager was immediately required to confirm the truth of his father's claim by repeating the aria "Nessun dorma". His voice, still undeveloped but fresh and clear, was favourably judged by everyone present. As a result of this performance, the Society's directors, Pradelli and Silingardi, placed him on the list of "first tenors."

Luciano was now officially one of a small group of Corale Rossini singers who, under the guidance of Maestro Livio Borri, would go on to win important competitions, including the international Llangollen competition in Wales.

The opera house was to provide Luciano with the opportunity to build on his brief experience as a choral singer. Maestro Borri was director of both the Corale Rossini and the Chorus of the Teatro Comunale. Naturally he enrolled the promising young tenor in the ranks of the opera chorus.

The musical professionalism of the chorus members was shaky to say the least. They came from a variety of backgrounds: there were farmers, shoemakers and greengrocers, together with the odd doctor and lawyer. Hardly any of them could read music. Poor Maestro Borri made heroic efforts to persuade them to work on their sight-reading, but resistance was stubborn, and a core of die-hards would refer scornfully to the musical notation as "those little black dots".

Thus Luciano's opera début took place among this ragbag of amateurs, in a very challenging opera: Arrigo Boito's *Mefistofele*. For the record, the

Pavarotti with his old friends from the Rossini Choral Society. (Photo Roncaglia)

Pavarotti with his father. (© 1989, Judith Kovacs)

conductor was Vincenzo Bellezza, the protagonist was Raffaele Arié, with Rosetta Noli and Luciano Panzieri as Margherita and Faust.

In a frenzy of applause the audience demanded an encore of the prologue, one of the most important parts of the opera. No doubt this unusual success was due in considerable measure to the voices of the two Pavarottis, who worked hard to bring some vigour to the rather lame chorus.

At its third performance, a matinée, Rosetta Noli was replaced by a young newcomer from Modena, Mirella Freni. She too was destined for a great career, and that day received an encore for her "L'altra notte in fondo al mare."

The two greatest singers that Modena has ever known failed to meet on that occasion, for the director had squeezed the whole choir into the narrow space below the stage. Luciano, in that absurd and awkward position, sweating profusely in the stifling heat, had to be content with hearing the protagonists' muffled voices from overhead, through the floorboards of the stage.

CHOOSING A TEACHER

A character as strong and decisive as Luciano could never be satisfied with a career as a choral singer. By now he was reaching the age when he would have to make the choices that would determine his future. He had just gained his elementary school teaching diploma, but although school teaching offered a secure and untroubled career, he did not find the idea particularly appealing.

His natural gifts of eloquence and empathy led him to take up a job in a different field – insurance. Seasoned professionals predicted a richly satisfying future for him. But his own instincts and his family *milieu* were inclining him ever more irresistibly towards a theatrical career. To a provincial lad with his feet firmly planted on the ground, this prospect, exciting as it was, seemed fraught with unpredictability and uncertainty.

Luciano began to look around cautiously with a view to making one of the hardest and most delicate decisions facing someone who is about to devote himself to the study of singing: the choice of a teacher. To generic term "teacher" is not in fact very precise. In reality the pupil nearly always needs two teachers: a so-called *vocalista* or "voice coach" (generally an ex-singer) who can pass on the secrets of vocal technique; and another musician, known generically and somewhat simplistically as a "score teacher" (*maestro di spartito*) who has in-depth knowledge of the opera repertoire.

It is not easy to find a combination of these qualities in a single person, even though the definitions of the two types of teacher are quite elastic. In Modena at that time no such figure existed.

Luciano, rightly, began to look for a voice coach first; when he felt more experienced and skilful vocally he could think about finding a score teacher.

The most capable voice coaches working in Modena at the time were: Luigi Bertazzoni, a baritone highly regarded in the first half of the century, whose pupil Mirella Freni was now starting to enjoy some success, and who had also taught Arrigo Pola; Vincenzo Guicciardi from Modena, another ageing baritone from the same era as Bertazzoni, whose school never produced any particularly distinguished pupils, and whose teaching therefore aroused considerable scepticism; Anny Veronesi, an ex-mezzo-soprano with a *basso profondo* voice resulting from 120 cigarettes a day, who did not inspire much confidence; and the trunk-maker Dante Arcelli, who had discovered his niece Mirella's precocious talent, and was just now starting to make his mark.

All things considered, however, only Bertazzoni offered a guaranteed level of competence and professionalism. There was just one problem: because of his advanced years this elderly teacher would often doze off at the piano during lessons.

Following his instincts, Luciano now made a brave choice which proved to be very shrewd; he chose not an ex-singer but someone with an active singing career, albeit nearing its decline: Arrigo Pola.

The people of Modena felt ambivalent towards Pola. They could hardly fail to admire the unique and almost angelic tone-quality of this tenor's voice in *Faust* at La Scala, or his *Traviata* with Maria Callas at the Teatro Regio in Parma. On the other hand his fellow citizens disliked his rather proud demeanour, which could easily be construed as arrogance. In fact this brilliant singer put on his bravado as a means of concealing his anxiety and insecurity in the face of such eminent colleagues as Beniamino Gigli, Ferruccio Tagliavini and Giuseppe Di Stefano.

Pola had just returned to Italy after a long stay in Japan, where he enjoyed widespread popularity. His wife Margherita informed him that two gentlemen, Fernando and Luciano Pavarotti, wanted an audition with him. Tired and unsettled after his long journey, he would have preferred to postpone this unexpected task, but the two men were firmly installed in the lobby with no apparent intention of leaving.

When Margherita gently tried to suggest they come back on another day, they replied that they would be happy to wait until the Maestro had rested.

So Pola reluctantly opened the piano and called in the younger man, who seemed to be about eighteen years old. After only a few vocal exercises, Pola realised that he was in the presence of an exceptional talent.

Luciano could comfortably reach top E flat, three semitones above top C – the furthest limit of most tenors' vocal range.

What struck Pola was the fact that the high notes were not in falsetto or "half-voice"; even the E flat resounded in full voice, with that unique, exciting and mysterious effect that the human voice can have when it is employed at the very limit of its powers.

Pola's fatigue gave way to a state of excitement and euphoria; it seemed incredible to him that such a young lad, with hardly any training, could display such natural fluency and ease of production. He asked Luciano to sing an *a capella* (unaccompanied) aria, and this time the young man's natural and instinctive phrasing in "Ch'ella mi creda" convinced Pola that here was someone of unique ability, to be nurtured with the utmost attention.

For about two years Pola lovingly cultivated Luciano's technique, with vocal exercises focused on agility, sustained notes, octave jumps and arpeggios. He also taught Luciano a wide variety of songs with the help of Tiziana Dondi Levrini, a piano teacher who sometimes assisted him with his lessons.

Even though his outstanding pupil later modified and perfected Pola's breathing technique (founded on contracting the diaphragm inwards), Pola deserves recognition for the care with which he treated that young voice during the most delicate phase of its development.

Then there came a point at which the young tenor's artistic needs were no longer satisfied by lessons based almost exclusively on vocal exercises. Driven by his compelling desire to build a solid musical foundation, he requested an audition with me.

Although, as I said, Modena had (supposedly) quite a few voice coaches, I was the only score teacher. To tell the truth, I regarded this activity as a hobby or temporary means of earning some money; my aspirations were largely set on becoming a concert pianist and conductor. However I found it impossible to refuse the continual requests I received from singing teachers who were completely illiterate musically and desperately needed a musician who could improve their pupils' poor sight-reading.

So, from the age of fourteen, I moved between the so-called "schools" run by Arcelli, Veronesi and Bertazzoni. The latter seemed to me by far the best qualified. He was also a distant relative, my mother's uncle. I was fascinated by his stories about his opera career. I could listen for hours as he talked of bygone singers I had never heard of, whom he described as legendary, inimitable – the tenors Gubellini, Bussetti, Tincani; the sopranos Lina Bruna Rasa, Celestina Boninsegna, Elena Rakowska; or others, better-known because they were more recent, such as Carlo Galeffi and Titta Ruffo. He had sung with them all.

I was particularly intrigued by tales of his friendship with Enrico Caruso, with whom he had sung many times. I listened to many curious anecdotes about this great Neapolitan tenor, such as the one about him almost always failing to pitch the last high note correctly in "La donna è mobile". Other stories were more edifying: Caruso was, it seems, a remarkably generous man, lending money to Bertazzoni who was rather improvident in his youth, as well as in later years.

Whenever I asked him to describe the colour of Caruso's voice, the old tutor's sullen expression would become serene and almost dreamy. "Indescribable, my dear, indescribable!" he would say. "It was velvet, yes, the velvet of that voice was indescribable…" And Bertazzoni, usually such a talkative and expansive man, would suddenly be speechless, his eyes misty with emotion.

Soon, however, he would regain his fighting spirit. To make us forget that emotional moment he would invariably tell us how Caruso had solved the problem of breathing support (every singer's nightmare and delight) by pushing exactly as you do when seated on the lavatory!

I was developing an enviable knowledge of the opera repertoire through Bertazzoni's teachings and tales, as well as my daily work with his pupils. Among these were Mirella Freni, who was later to become my wife, and indeed Arrigo Pola, then at the peak of his fine career. I was still in short trousers when I taught him a great many operas: *Lohengrin, Andrea Chénier, Adriana Lecouvreur, Un ballo in maschera…*

By the time I was twenty I could play, from memory, nearly all the most frequently performed operas. And that is when Luciano came looking for me.

Pesaro 1954. On Luciano's left are his mother and sister.

1952, Luciano in the Lepanto football team.

MY MEETING WITH LUCIANO PAVAROTTI

I was twenty when I first met Luciano. He was nineteen, and by chance I had heard him sing a few days before we met, in his first ever television appearance. The state broadcasting service RAI had organised a series of transmissions from all over Italy. The aim was to promote the use of television, still in its infancy. The series was open to amateur performers in every field.

Mirella and I, recently married, had also been asked to take part in the show, which was to be broadcast exclusively in Modena and its province. After lengthy discussions we had decided, somewhat snobbishly, to refuse RAI's invitation. "Good grief," we had replied on the telephone, "we're established artists! How dare you put us in the category of amateurs?"

Even so, we sat down to watch. We wanted to be sure that the standard of this programme was indeed low enough to justify our proud but painful refusal. We also felt that constant, secret fear, common to all artists, young and old, that out of those hordes of hopefuls there might emerge a pianist or a soprano capable of jeopardising our professional supremacy within the city. There we were, about to watch the début of a young tenor, and Mirella was telling me a curious story about him.

"His name is Luciano Pavarotti," she was saying, "and we're milk-siblings."

Feeling rather drowsy from watching this tedious programme, I failed to grasp the exact meaning of "milk-siblings", and Mirella's detailed explanation had further soporific effects on me.

"Luciano is the son of my mother's best friend, Adele Pavarotti. Neither his mother nor mine had any milk, and Luciano and I were breast-fed by the same wet-nurse. In those days there was no powdered milk. Anyway they wouldn't have had enough money to buy it…"

Her explanation was interrupted by the announcement of "Nessun dorma" from Puccini's *Turandot*, and a tenor with a very youthful, smiling face attacked the opening phrases with great aplomb. The young man's voice impressed me immediately. It was of course somewhat light for the piece, but it rang out as bright and clear as silver. At the point where the melody begins its hazardous climb up the rungs of the stave, his voice, rather than straining, acquired greater tone, reaching and sustaining the last high note with effortless ease.

My torpor gave way to excitement – the kind that one feels when witnessing an extraordinary event without being fully aware of it.

I was one of the very few people to witness Luciano Pavarotti's television début – at that time only a few dozen televisions had been sold in Modena – and it has not been mentioned in any biography. I found it very hard to get to sleep that night. That voice, so clear and natural, had given me a rush of adrenalin that took several hours to disperse.

A few days later, on an appointment made by his mother, I received him at my studio in Via Rua Muro, one of the oldest and most beautiful streets in Modena's historic centre.

I liked him immediately for his uninhibited and open-hearted manner. He begged me to give him my honest opinion of his artistic prospects, explaining that he had not yet decided which path to follow – insurer, elementary school teacher, or singer. He then proceeded to perform "Tombe degli avi miei", from *Lucia di Lammermoor*.

I was concerned that the microphones might have made his voice sound better than it was, as they often do. But as I listened to the opening bars of the recitative, delivered with such clean, smooth phrasing, I realised with pleasure that his voice sounded even better live than on television. True, there was the odd musical or rhythmic inaccuracy; but wasn't this precisely why he had come to me?

His performance of that difficult aria, in the original key (many tenors, even famous ones, regularly take the entire final act of *Lucia* a semitone lower) confirmed my impression that this was someone out of the ordinary.

I expressed my admiration unreservedly, which pleased Luciano. However, I also stressed his need for more serious, in-depth musical studies. He replied enthusiastically, "Let's start right away. I want to prepare for some singing competitions, and I don't want to miss a single day of study."

We worked strenuously for many months. I soon realised, from the way he resisted submitting to the iron rules of sight-singing, that his natural musicality could not, and possibly should not, be completely subdued.

Luciano would listen carefully as I demonstrated a musical phrase with the correct rhythmic and dynamic values; then he would repeat it, with slight variations and with various idiosyncratic shadings, sometimes in sharp contrast to the composer's directions.

We argued frequently about what I felt was his excessive freedom of interpretation. Over the years I came to believe that this tendency of his

Studying with Leone Magiera. (Photo Studio De Bon)

almost to rewrite the music was, when not carried to excess, the expression of a very powerful, effusive personality.

In fact the phrasing of great singers is hardly ever strictly confined to the composer's notation; the very word "interpret" implies that each performer must bring to the composition that breath of life that carries the hallmark of his or her unique talent.

Certainly, working with Pavarotti was not always easy for conductors and pianists. They needed exceptional imagination and quick reflexes. His endless discovery of the music, always performing it as if for the first time, could pose serious problems for fellow artists, but it made the music always seem fresh, alive and thrilling, with never a moment's lowering of tension.

Our work was not confined to the study of scores; due to my experience of working with the "voice coaches" of Modena, I was also able to have long discussions with Luciano about vocal matters. In between her early tours, Mirella Freni, who had also studied with Pola and Bertazzoni, often joined in our investigations and discussions, contributing significantly with her ideas and experience.

Freni was already sharing the stage with some of the greatest singers of the time: Elizabeth Schwarzkopf, Sesto Bruscantini, Geraint Evans, Luigi Alva… She diligently picked up technical tips from them all, and would pass these on to us with a wealth of detail. From these long study sessions as a threesome, we found ourselves enriched by new, stimulating experiences.

FURTHER STUDIES AND COMPETITIONS

For some time Mirella and I had, with Bertazzoni's grudging consent, been travelling regularly to Mantova for lessons with a well-known teacher, Ettore Campogalliani. He was much talked about. Wee knew he had taught Renata Tebaldi, Aldo Protti, Flaviano Labò and Piero Cappuccilli among others. His pupils continued to win prizes in singing competitions – by virtue, no doubt, of his excellent tuition.

Luciano was very interested in our accounts of these lessons, and I could see that he wanted to join in. I suspect that financial concerns were holding him back – a lesson cost two thousand lire, a considerable sum at that time.

Finally he decided to give it a go, and one day we set off for Mantova, all together in my first car, a tiny sputtering Bianchi that I was extremely proud of. In those days Mirella and Luciano (particularly Luciano) were young, full of hope and high spirits. With the windows down, oblivious to the draughts, they gave a joyous display of vocal exercises and songs that made people turn in amazement as we passed through the charming little towns of Carpi, Novi and San Benedetto Po, on the road between Modena and Mantova.

Luciano had to go through an audition – really a small musical exam – before he could join these classes. Campogalliani would not take everyone who came forward. Although we had given him the best possible account of our friend, his personal approval was required for admission to the course.

The maestro was greatly impressed with Luciano's voice. I had mentioned discreetly that the lad was not blessed with huge wealth, and he decided to offer him a considerable discount on the price of lessons.

For several years all three of us attended Campogalliani's courses. After my piano diploma I had also gained a diploma in teaching singing, so I was extremely keen to find out the pedagogical secrets of the last of the great "voice-wizards".

We always spent several hours in the enormous waiting room, seated among the small crowd of pupils waiting their turn. From the maestro's studio, separated from us only by a glass door, we could hear every student's efforts quite clearly. Campogalliani's frequent, colourful interruptions, almost always in Mantovan dialect, provoked amusing comments from this informal audience. Often his mother, a pleasant, active woman in her nineties, would appear and ask us kindly not to make too much noise.

The length of these lessons varied wildly. If the pupil was slow on the uptake and failed to satisfy the teacher's demands, the lesson was over in a few minutes. When our turn came, Mirella and Luciano would get about an hour each. We often had joint lessons, and Campogalliani would frequently ask me to take his place at the piano. As a former concert pianist, he was able to teach piano as well as voice. He maintained that the piano accompanist, having to act as a substitute for a large orchestra, needed to produce the same tone and colour as an orchestra. He expected me, therefore, to have perfect knowledge of the instrumentation of every piece I played, and if I played an oboe solo too forcefully, or a horn solo too fast, he would reprimand me indignantly.

Consequently I got into the habit of studying both the vocal and orchestral scores of the pieces Mirella and Luciano were performing. This habit has stayed with me, and I strongly recommend it to young pianists who intend to devote themselves to the art of accompaniment.

A kind of hierarchy of time had developed among that crowd of pupils. While Gabriella, the granddaughter of the famous conductor Ettore Panizza, rarely achieved more than fifteen minutes' of lesson time, Renza Jotti, Dmitri Nabokov and Bianca Bellesia only got ten minutes each. A few steps higher up was a trio consisting of John Allen, Raffaella Ferrari and Carlo Menippo, who each enjoyed the privilege of half an hour. Not surprisingly, the forty-five minutes or more granted to Mirella and Luciano provoked glances of admiration mixed with envy as they emerged from the holy of holies.

Luciano particularly liked the tenor voices of Menippo and Allen. But Menippo's extraordinary beauty of tone was inversely proportionate to his musical aptitude, while Allen's enviable vocal ability was diminished by its lack of power and feeling.

As time went by we came to understand that Campogalliani was not just an excellent voice coach, but also a brilliant teacher of music. He undoubtedly achieved superb vocal results, but almost always starting from a more psychological than technical point of view: he influenced the singer's frame of mind, stimulating the imagination with extremely skilful and ingenious advice about interpretation.

For example, when Luciano first sang him "Che gelida manina" he was troubled by the repeated A flats at the start, which are rather low for a tenor. He tried to boost the sound artificially, but the maestro explained that he would never have achieved his own success if he had concentrated on technique alone.

"You need to be as moved as Rodolfo," he told him, "when he takes Mimi's hand for the first time. Don't think of anything else, only this, and you'll see that your voice will respond in the right way."

And suddenly those A flats, previously so awkward, came pouring forth full of dramatic atmosphere and pathos.

In teaching his idiosyncratic and very effective "technique of no technique", Campogalliani undoubtedly had the advantage of being able to choose the best pupils who had studied hardest; these lessons really were *lezioni di perfezionamento* – "lessons in perfection".

Nevertheless, the importance of artistic inspiration for improving technique, a topic I will discuss further in the appendices, is an idea I have often heard forcefully propounded by the great Maestri: Alfred Cortot, David Oistrakh, Herbert Von Karajan and Franco Ferrara.

Luciano was at the point in his studies where his vocal and musical grounding, already solid and secure, needed perfecting. On the surface, then, it might seem that Campogalliani's task was not too complicated. In fact, the final touches to a work of art are the most difficult, and the lessons Luciano received from the maestro of Mantova were crucial for providing artistic polish and, at a psychological level, for developing his emotional and moral strength.

He put an end to Luciano's misuse of *portamenti* (the singing of two distant notes by dragging the voice), which was typical of the old school. He also taught him to give his utmost concentration to the piece he was singing.

"Every fall in emotional tension," he would say, "is like a large smear on a painting by Mantegna."

While on the subject of the great painter, he suggested that Luciano should visit the renowned Camera degli Sposi in the Ducal Palace and all the other artistic treasures in Mantova, maintaining that an opera singer should be widely cultured and open to all forms of art.

Musically, he urged Luciano not to limit himself to listening to the opera repertoire, indispensable though this was, but to include chamber and symphonic works.

Such ideas were relatively new and daring in those days, when opera singers were renowned – rightly or wrongly – for their ignorance and narrow-mindedness, and when singing teachers were simply expected to come up with miracle prescriptions for the use of the diaphragm and the "mask". Luciano treasured this valuable advice, and subsequently lost no opportunity to go to symphonic concerts and even to orchestra rehearsals, which he rightly regarded as deeply interesting experiments in interpretation as well as a means of staying culturally up to date.

It was not uncommon to come across him in the grand concert halls; at the end of Vladimir Horowitz's last performance at Scala I saw him, deeply moved, kissing the hands of the great pianist.

Campogalliani also knew how to guide his pupils in their first steps as artists, almost in the spirit of a manager. He knew the tortuous paths of the Italian opera world like the back of his hand. He always knew whom to telephone to arrange an audition, which journalist to contact for a review or a feature article, who was the best theatre agent for a particular repertoire.

Luciano began to realise that to build a successful career you need more than artistic talent, indispensable as that is; you also have to make intelligent moves and trust the right people.

He began to look around for a manager – known in the theatre as an "agent" – who could help him along the road to success.

There were plenty of theatre agents on the opera scene, who would occasionally turn themselves into impresarios. But the really good ones were barely a handful: Ansaloni, Barosi, Finzi and Liduino Bonardi, always known simply as Liduino.

Mirella Freni had recently joined Ada Finzi, Liduino's ex-secretary, who was perhaps the most intellectual and refined of this group of agents. She had some important European festivals "in the bag", as they say: Aix-en-Provence, Glyndebourne, and the Holland Festival. The youthful Freni was just the right singer for this repertoire, and seemed well placed to take over from Graziella Sciutti, now advanced in years, as "Queen of the Piccola Scala" (La Scala's touring company).

Freni was keen that her "milk-brother" should join the same agency, and Finzi would have been delighted to take him on. But Luciano, who was evidently becoming fully aware of his abilities and his prospects, sought to defer his decision as long as possible. He was convinced that his voice was becoming more suitable for grand opera: *Bohème, Butterfly, Traviata, Rigoletto*. All these operas were regularly organised by Liduino, not Finzi, who specialized more in Mozart or the more rarefied and élite works, such as *Il matrimonio segreto*, or *Falstaff*.

He decided, then, that Liduino was the right man to approach. He set off for an audition in the company of Arrigo Pola, who knew the famous

Milanese impresario well, having worked for his organisation for many years.

On that day that Luciano faced his first serious problem as a tenor.

For some time he had been aware that now and again, right in the middle of a song, his voice would suddenly become hoarse, only to return after an hour or so, full and clear as if nothing had happened. He was quite seriously worried by this problem, which had occurred so far only within the four forgiving walls of my studio, or at Campogalliani's. It had never caused serious difficulties in his first public concerts.

Arrigo Pola had introduced him to Liduino in fulsome terms, using plenty of colourful language and describing him as *un tenore lungo* – "a long tenor", with the C, C sharp and even D natural "under his belt".

Momentarily, the elderly agent's cold, avaricious face had seemed to form itself into a kind of smile. For him those tenor high notes represented tinkling coins, and in his heart he hoped that Pola's extravagant words would be well founded.

With youthful boldness Luciano began to sing "Che gelida manina". The moving entry of Puccini's famous aria, and the following resplendent B flat in the phrase "Chi son", fired Pola's enthusiasm. He fidgeted continuously in his chair, barely able to restrain himself from interrupting his pupil's performance with inopportune exclamations of delight.

Even Liduino's shark's eyes seemed to light up as the performance continued, ever more fluent and touching.

Suddenly, disaster: the A flat in "Talor, dal mio forziere" stuck in his throat, producing an unexpected and jarring false note. Pola's face went white; he gripped the arms of his chair.

Liduino reacted violently: he shot up and left, slamming the door and muttering that he had no need for "short" tenors and time-wasters.

Luciano, more shocked than humiliated, found words of comfort and encouragement from Alessandro Ziliani, a tenor famous in the first half of the century, who was soon to take over the agency.

He returned to Modena, worried about the recurrence of this puzzling problem, which he preferred not to talk about too much, even with his closest and most trusted friends. He had started smoking the odd cigarette, but as soon as he suspected that it might be responsible for what was happening, he gave up this dangerous vice.

It is quite probable that Dr Alvaro Magnoni diagnosed a form of pharyngitis – Luciano did not reveal this to anyone – but on more than one occasion he took himself off to Terme della Salvarola, a small spa town near Sassuolo, for a course of treatment.

This treatment proved successful; his problem occurred less frequently, and disappeared completely after a few years.

Meanwhile Finzi, maybe because she had heard about his misfortune with Liduino, was once again offering to represent him. Luciano continued to wait; he was always very resolute in the decisions he made, and fortunately they almost always proved to be the right ones.

He had high hopes for his next singing competition: the Achille Peri in Reggio Emilia. This was still quite newly established but its winners had quickly made a name for themselves. Among them was Mirella Freni.

Also, the quality of the judges was guaranteed. They were professionals at the highest level, many of them golden names in the history of opera: Mafalda Favero, one of the most popular and well-loved sopranos of the first half of the twentieth century; Maria Zamboni, who had sung the role of Liù in the first performance of *Turandot*, directed by Toscanini at La Scala; Mariano Stabile, perhaps the most famous Falstaff of all time; Giulia Tess, the first Italian Salomè in Strauss's opera of the same name. Influential musicians such as Giulio Confalonieri and Ettore Campogalliani made up the rest of this illustrious panel of judges.

I was the official pianist for the competition, so Luciano had none of the problems of adapting to the accompanist which sometimes crop up in this kind of singing contest, where the sheer number of competitors makes it almost impossible to rehearse with the pianist, even for a few minutes beforehand.

We had been rehearsing the selected pieces almost daily, and his problem seemed to have disappeared completely. His voice was back on top form. Luciano performed confidently and resolutely in the elimination rounds, sailing through them without any problems. In fact, Campogalliani had revealed to me in confidence that Luciano had the highest overall score. The only singer capable of snatching victory from him was John Allen; he was second in the ranking, but some distance behind. Barring an unforeseen event, Luciano was all set to win.

On the evening of the final, which was open to the public, all the remaining competitors were showing signs of nervous strain, apart from Luciano, who looked steady and controlled.

Years later, my hands can still feel the weight I put into the dramatic, unexpected ninth chord, and the simultaneous melody played by the third and fourth fingers of the right hand, which mark the beginning of "Ah! Fuyez, douce image", Des Grieux's aria in the St. Sulpice scene from *Manon* by Massenet.

Luciano had chosen this piece, still generally performed in Italian ("Ah, dispar vision"), to prove to himself and others that he had the stamina for an aria as long and as difficult as this. He responded to the brief but fiery piano introduction with an attack so full of intensity and pathos on the words "Io son sol. Solo alfin. Il gran momento è questo" ("I am alone! Alone at the last! This is the great moment!"), that I had to force myself to stay calm and detached. His voice, so rich and expressive, threatened to overwhelm me.

The performance seemed to be going beautifully. We were approaching the first of two vocal pitfalls: in both cases the melodic line finds its way up to some B flats which are difficult because of the preceding *tessitura* (of repeated Gs and A flats) and the tense and agonising drama of the song.

Suddenly I noticed a chink in Luciano's vocal armour; apparently the old problem was back, at the worst possible moment, playing havoc with the first series of B flats, which sounded tight and dull.

I felt icy beads of sweat running down the sides of my body, and, throwing him a quick glance, I could see his distress.

Nevertheless, he carried on bravely. The low, middle and passing

Hamburg, March 1989. (© 1989, Judith Kovacs)

registers did not seem to be compromised, and Luciano still had a chance to redeem himself with the repeat of the difficult phrase. But the second time, as though in a nightmare, the high register just refused to function, and the climb up to those terrifying B flats seemed as steep as a sheer rock face.

Still, he carried on to the end, his face distorted by anger and exertion. As he left the stage the knowledgeable audience applauded him for his overall qualities, in spite of what had befallen him.

He knew that victory was slipping out of his grasp. Earlier John Allen had given a convincing rendition of "Nessun dorma", and after a long discussion the judges awarded the first prize in the category of "tenor voices" to the American.

Mafalda Favero went up on stage to hand out the prizes, and I realised then, from the furious expression on Luciano's face as he received his silver medal, what kind of man he was: second place was not for him.

HIS DÉBUT AT LAST

The period that followed the Peri competion was not a happy one for Luciano. After his unfortunate audition with Liduino, this was the second serious blow to his professional pride. To make matters worse, Finzi had gone silent, possibly annoyed by his failure to give her a firm answer.

At this difficult time Mirella, Campogalliani and I tried everything to help him out of the crisis of discouragement that gripped him. For some weeks he shut himself away at home and refused to speak to anyone.

When he came back into circulation we did our best to persuade him to start making concert appearances again. These were concerts of opera arias with piano accompaniment – as unpopular with the critics as they were useful for the professional development of a young singer.

Campogalliani was often asked to organise such evenings, even in minor towns like Carpi, Rubiera, Fabbrico, Sermide and San Benedetto Po. This great man, whom we admired so much that we called him simply "the Maestro", was not above sitting down at the piano (which he played magnificently) to accompany his best pupils at these concerts.

And so Luciano made his comeback in one of these small towns. Mirella insisted on being there with him on the first night, even though she herself was by now appearing in much more prestigious venues.

The audiences may have been unsophisticated but they were full of enthusiasm, and they soon restored Luciano's morale. He began to look forward to winning the Peri gold medal next time around.

An important change was announced for the 1961 Peri Competition: the winners would be offered a full-scale début, with a real orchestra and well-known conductors, in addition to the purely symbolic medals and certificates. Apart from this there were no significant changes. The panel was still robust – Favero, Stabile, Zamboni, Tess, Confalonieri and Campogalliani – all charming people with whom I spent many happy hours in the delightful little restaurants of Reggio, listening long past midnight to their tales of the glory days.

By then I felt very much at home in Reggio. I had gained much of my early experience as an assistant conductor in its splendid theatre, and once again I was to be the competition pianist, ready to play several hundred songs in the course of just three days.

It was a real *tour de force*, made more bearable by my friend Gianfranco Masini, and Luciano himself, who between them managed to get me to force down the odd panino on the rare occasions when the judges took longer than usual to discuss a contestant's merits.

Pavarotti, mindful of Campogalliani's precepts, did not miss a single moment of the competition. He was convinced that listening carefully to over a hundred young colleagues was an opportunity for professional development that was not to be missed. As the various auditions ended he would share with me his astute observations on the singers who impressed him most. The opinions of the judges almost invariably coincided with his.

When his turn came, the performance of one piece was enough to see him into the final round. He was first in the provisional rankings, as he had been last year.

The final evening of the competition was his first true moment of greatness. The theatre was already filled with fans from his concerts in the small provincial towns around Modena, Reggio and Mantova. He sang "Che gelida manina", placing a private symbolic claim on *Bohème*, which was rumoured to be one of the most likely operas for the winners' début.

For some time he had been working on a new technique which produced superb results in the hardest phrase of a song. In his continuous quest for vocal perfection, he had noticed that by squeezing the diaphragm to its utmost, thus emptying all the air from the lungs in the phrase preceding the C in "speranza", the next intake of breath was deeper and more complete, so he was in optimal condition for the difficulty ahead. When he sang "Poiché v'ha preso stanza" with the fullest possible breath and voice, the C in "speranza" would come out as never before, as long as he remained a little on the defensive in the preceding phrases. Armed with this new secret, he began singing this demanding piece.

It was an unforgettable performance – with just the right emotion in his voice at first, gradually becoming warmer and more passionate, and then with a pure, clear, strong C. The audience could not contain themselves: they erupted in wild applause before the aria had even finished.

The judges were in no doubt. Within minutes Mafalda Favero was onstage, holding the winner's gold medal in her hand. Clearly moved, she held Luciano in a long embrace.

Then Mariano Stabile, with the perfect aplomb of the Sicilian gentleman, repeated the phrase which, years before, the people of nearby

Parma had used to greet the victory of the young Beniamino Gigli in their competition: "Habemus Tenorem!" ("We have a Tenor!").

Luciano was ecstatic with joy.

We concluded that memorable evening with an equally memorable dinner in the company of the judges. At the end, on the restaurant's dilapidated piano, I accompanied a high-spirited Mariano Stabile (stoked by several bottles of Lambrusco) in a couple of extracts from *Falstaff*, which he sang with full voice and great artistic refinement, despite his very advanced age.

The rumours proved to be correct: *Bohème* was one of the operas chosen for the winners' début, and naturally Luciano was to sing the part of Rodolfo in every performance: two in Reggio Emilia and one in Modena.

I had been asked to conduct the performance in our city. It would also be my début in *Bohème* – with no rehearsals! My actual début as an orchestral conductor had taken place a few days before in Reggio Emilia, in *Suor Angelica*.

Among the famous names promised for the performances, the only important one was the Bolognese conductor Francesco Molinari Pradelli. Along with Antonino Votto, Gianandrea Gavazzeni, Vittorio Gui, Gabriele Santini, Nino Sanzogno and Oliviero de Fabritiis, he was one of the most highly regarded Italian conductors of the day. He was known, for his obstinacy and inflexibility, as a "*castiga cantanti*", a tormentor of singers. As a result Luciano and I worked extremely hard on the opera. Soon the rehearsals began.

Rather than stay in a hotel we would set off for Reggio each morning in my gasping little Bianchi, returning to Modena late at night. We had a small daily allowance for expenses from the Peri Competition, and made savings where we could. That short trip also gave us the chance to unwind after the long day's rehearsals.

Mafalda Favero had been given the task of directing the opera. Although she was a magnificent singer she had little experience as a director, and she tried to make up for this by rehearsing the same scene over and over again, often without managing to find a satisfactory solution. Fortunately Luciano's personal qualities were already starting to shine, and when the director got bogged down in some minor detail, he would suggest a solution, which Favero would immediately adopt, delighted at solving the problem so easily.

I have often wondered what became of Luciano's colleagues from those first performances: the sopranos Pellegrini, Giannotti, and Polina Savridi who all sang the role of Mimì; Bianca Bellesia and Renza Jotti as Musetta; the baritones Mattioli and De Ambrosis as Marcello and Schaunard. As far as I know, they all disappeared quite quickly from the operatic scene (Renza Jotti died very young). Only Nabokov Junior, who sang Colline, is still in the public eye, but as a novelist like his father, the well-known author of *Lolita*.

Molinari Pradelli arrived only a few days before the dress rehearsal. He knocked the ramshackle orchestra into shape, threatening to sack several musicians, but he was relatively lenient with the young singers. He even congratulated Luciano after the dress rehearsal – a rare compliment, given his reputation for stormy relationships with singers, even famous ones.

At last, with everyone in a state of more or less relaxed readiness, the curtain of the Teatro Comunale rose on 29th April 1961 for Luciano Pavarotti's début.

I had just finished a rehearsal of *Suor Angelica*. I arrived out of breath, just in time to slip into the stage-box. As the house lights were going down I recognised Alessandro Ziliani sitting at the front of the stalls. I assumed he was there because Favero was directing; it was rumoured that they had been very much in love in their youth. Then I realised just what his presence meant: Liduino, that hugely powerful theatrical agent, had recently passed away; Ziliani had taken his place, and from his office in Via Santa Radegonda he managed singers, conductors and directors, sending them out to all the most important theatres in the world.

Luciano embarked on a performance that was memorable from its opening lines: "Nei cieli bigi, vedo fumar dai mille comignoli, Parigi".

His voice had matured nicely. Up to now certain critics had claimed, with some justification, that it lacked volume and intensity of tone. That evening he proved them wrong, utterly and conclusively. From beginning to end, the assurance and ease of his marvellous tenor timbre reminded me of other great voices of the past: the captivating lustre of Jussi Björling, Mario Filippeschi's unforgettable high notes. The C in "speranza", the B natural of the *concertato* in the second act, the B flat in the third, were all moments of delight for the audience. When the opera ended they awarded him triumphal honours with the most indescribable pandemonium.

Some people were crying, some were waving their handkerchiefs like flags, others were shouting his name. Luciano, happy as a child, was thanking them with sweeping gestures, also moved to tears – he certainly wasn't expecting such frenzy.

I struggled through the hordes of new fans, dragging Ziliani, who seemed to be in a state of shock; he kept repeating, as if in a trance, the same two words: "Jussi Björling, Jussi Björling."

When we reached the dressing room it was Luciano's turn to be shocked. Ziliani had recovered the power of speech, and was proclaiming loudly (and with admirable foresight) that he wished to bow down before the greatest tenor in the world.

Bologna, July 1989. (© 1989, Judith Kovacs)

THE EARLY YEARS OF HIS CAREER

Although it is undoubtedly hard for a young singer to bring the long years of study to fruition in a successful début, it is probably even more difficult, in the years that follow, to keep his or her vocal gift intact, preserving it through shrewd and prudent management.

The first and greatest danger is that, inevitably, the singer will be offered operatic roles that are beyond his or her powers at that particular time. If the young singer, new to the life of the theatre, fails to make the right choices, there is a risk of damaging the developing voice with a repertoire that is too demanding. Ziliani was familiar with this danger. He and Pavarotti meticulously agreed on a schedule which by today's standards would be considered about mid-range. For three or four years he did not hazard a single step outside the classical repertory of the pure lyric tenor: *Bohème*, *Traviata*, *Rigoletto*, *Butterfly*; occasionally he was allowed *Lucia di Lammermoor*, as long as he followed advice not to sing too loudly in the dramatic marriage scene.

Ziliani, who was developing an almost paternal fondness for Luciano, always telephoned me, Pola and Campogalliani for our approval of this work schedule. We all found it sensible and well-planned. We agreed that Pavarotti should be given plenty of time to prepare this repertoire. In fact, he spent six months of study before returning to the stage after his début in Reggio. When he did return it was once again in his favourite *Bohème*, with Rosanna Carteri as Mimì, at the Teatro del Giglio in Lucca. There he received the warmest congratulations from the great Tito Schipa, whom he had always admired and listened to with total attention.

By this time he had also finished studying *Rigoletto*, and on 1st November 1961 Luciano made his *Rigoletto* début on the familiar stage of the small but delightful Teatro Comunale in Carpi. Mafalda Favero and Alessandro Ziliani were in the stalls, enraptured by his performance.

For a tenor, this opera by Verdi represents a milestone. The Duke of Mantova's part is built on a vocal *tessitura* centred mainly on notes in the zone of transition between registers. Unless the covered-sound technique has been mastered (see technical appendix no. 3), there is no chance that the voice will be fresh when it comes to all the B flats and B naturals.

Luciano, mindful of the problems he had encountered and overcome in *Rigoletto*, always advised young tenors to study this opera. Even though his début had been an outstanding success, he pondered for years as to how to improve a number of moments in the role. One of these is the initial G flat in "Parmi veder le lacrime".

In his opinion, rightly, the first vowel of the aria was so open and important, being on the first note, that it required the correct pronunciation of the "a", although optimal delivery of the sound, G flat, required a closed vowel. After many performances he resolved the dilemma by using a mixed sound, half-way between "a" and "o".

Another problem was the final B natural in "La donna è mobile". Discussing this with him, I remembered a story I had heard from Bertazzoni (who by this time had died while a resident at the Casa Verdi in Milan). He had often mentioned that Enrico Caruso had exactly the same problem with that note.

In the end Luciano found the right vocal position when Tullio Serafin suggested he should perform the cadenza ending on a high C sharp – the bold solution once adopted by Giacomo Lauri Volpi. Thanks to the vocal position needed to produce the C sharp, the immediately following B natural came out with such ringing clarity and ease on the stage of Palermo's Teatro Massimo in 1962 that Pavarotti never forgot it. And whenever he was prevented from using Lauri Volpi's cadenza by the whim of some conductor less tolerant than Serafin, he still managed to maintain the equilibrium of the laryngeal muscles necessary to produce the difficult high note.

The third opera in his repertoire was *Traviata*, barely a month after *Rigoletto*, in accordance with the work schedule established by Ziliani.

Most of the major difficulties in the role of Alfredo are problems of intonation. The orchestral accompaniment to the tenor's melody is very thin, and often consists merely of weak pizzicati by the strings, making it hard for the orchestra's sound to reach the stage. This drawback can be prevented these days by amplifying the orchestral sound through loudspeakers in the wings, behind the singers. But in the Sixties such technical expedients did not exist, and the unfortunate tenors would be singing virtually *a cappella*, without instrumental accompaniment, in the most difficult passages, such as "Un dì, felice, eterea" or "Parigi, o cara".

Compassionate assistance from a deputy conductor concealed in the wings rarely improved matters. Usually in fact this made them worse, for the harmonium was never perfectly in tune with the orchestra's A.

I remember witnessing even famous tenors going through dreadfully bad times in their battle with the role of Alfredo, so I was anxious about the outcome of Luciano's début, in his first performance abroad, at the National Theatre in Belgrade, on 3rd December 1961, with Virginia Zeani co-starring. Knowing his infallible ear, however, I was not surprised when he told me the performance had been a success.

His perfect intonation amazed his colleagues and astonished the critics; *La traviata* became his *pièce de résistance* for several years. So it would have continued to be, if his meteoric career had not led him to abandon Alfredo, which is unfortunately considered a minor role for a tenor, and less rewarding than the soprano and baritone roles.

His last performance of the opera took place in October 1970 at the Metropolitan in New York. It is a real pity that younger opera lovers have not had the chance to hear his Alfredo in a live performance. Pavarotti made him a young, dashing, passionate character, not at all like the former stereotyped versions that had reduced Alfredo to a rather insipid and dramatically weak figure.

The chronological record of the early years of his career contains, alongside *Traviata*, an incredible series of performances of *Rigoletto* and *Bohème*. Pavarotti attributed the merit of having perfected his technique and developed his voice to *Rigoletto* in particular.

Although his early career was hugely rewarding, it was not without difficulties. Relationships with his work colleagues were not always idyllic. His first clash was with Ettore Gracis who conducted *Traviata* in Belgrade. Gracis was what one might call a serious professional, well-prepared and scrupulous. He was one of Benedetti Michelangeli's favourite conductors and, like this great pianist from Brescia, was committed to a perfect, even pedantic, organization of the work. This led, however, to a loss of that imagination and spontaneity of execution which sets great performers apart.

Pavarotti's artistic personality, passionate and inspirational, was ill-matched with Gracis, who was so precise and dogmatic. Sparks were bound to fly, only to be forgotten later (as almost always happens in the world of art) in the warm glow of the show's success.

From the very beginning Pavarotti had understood the need to protect and affirm his artistic personality. A conductor without exceptional interpretative abilities sometimes has the power to dull and restrict the singer's imagination, something which Pavarotti always vigorously refused to succumb to.

The claws of this young eagle were growing fast, as Molinari Pradelli discovered during rehearsals for *Rigoletto* at the Teatro Carlo Felice in

Milan, La Scala Opera Season 1965/66: Rigoletto – *With conductor Francesco Molinari-Pradelli. (© E. Piccagliani)*

Genova. When he scolded him brusquely and inopportunely regarding a "run" in the duet with Gilda in the first act, Luciano gave as good as he got. Only the timely intervention of the Superintendent, Celeste Lanfranco, prevented the argument from degenerating further.

His relationship with Molinari Pradelli, the conductor at his début, was always rather strained. It was to reach breaking point, as we shall see later, in the 1974 production of *La favorita* at the Teatro Comunale in Bologna.

Well aware by now of his prospects, and sure of his abilities, he coped brilliantly with a very difficult evening at the Teatro Comunale in Piacenza. He had been called in to replace a tenor from Piacenza, who had been sacked during rehearsals for *Rigoletto*. The local singer's fans were displeased with this decision, which had been made by the theatre management and the conductor. They were threatening to sabotage the performance.

As always happens in these situations, the nervous atmosphere ends up affecting all the performers, diminishing their powers.

At the first signs of protest from the disrupters, Giulio Fioravanti, in the lead role, began to falter, singing well below his normal standard, thus provoking further slings and arrows from the rabble.

Margherita Guglielmi, usually a very confident and captivating Gilda, was quite alarmed by the insults emanating from the upper gallery. Her final cadenza in "Caro nome" did not have its usual spontaneity, and the outcry grew louder, with the clear intention of unnerving Pavarotti as well – the ultimate target of the protest. Until that moment he was the only one to have been totally unaffected by the electric atmosphere, singing with his customary boldness, confidence and beauty of sound.

If it is true to say that a group of forty or fifty well-organised people can ruin a performance, it is equally true that if the majority of the audience directs its encouragement and affection towards the artist who manages to keep his nerve, then the performance can be a success.

This is precisely what happened with Luciano. In his difficult duet with Gilda, having already given a superb rendering of "Questa o quella", he had pitched a final D flat that had delighted the audience in the stalls. Then "Parmi veder le lacrime" met with applause so loud as to drown out instantly any attempt at intimidation.

The agitators in the upper gallery, forced into silence, held a council of war during the interval. One of them, Dal Fabbro, a part-time pharmacy student and well-known local prankster, was famous in Piacenza for his ability to belch on demand. He could swallow enormous quantities of air which he then unleashed with a tremendous roar. Since whistles, insults and hisses had failed to curb the young tenor's success, it was decided to resort to Dal Fabbro's deafening and vulgar "speciality".

The best moment for striking the defenceless adversary was chosen: the moment of silence that follows the last high note in "La donna è mobile". It is only a split-second, in which one sudden cry of "Bravo" can cause the entire audience to break into applause, as every experienced fan well knows. Conversely, one whistle or insult can produce quite the opposite effect.

The warlike Luciano was fully engaged in the final aria. He knew that once "La donna è mobile" was vanquished, final victory was assured. Reaching the final cadenza which, as we know, was not an easy task, even for someone with such fresh and sparkling vocal powers as his, he finished it in style with a long and exquisite B natural.

The loud, obscene roar emanating from the upper gallery left everyone dumbfounded: for a second there was utter silence, nobody could believe their ears. Luciano was the first to recover from the shock: with an imperious gesture he gave the start signal for the quartet, and everything continued as though nothing had happened.

While the tenor was giving a splendid rendition of "Bella figlia dell'amore", the majority of the audience decided to react to the vulgar insult with an ovation at the end of the quartet which was positively triumphal.

Pavarotti had shown his ability to command a rowdy audience, and news of his success that night in the face of such hostility soon reached Milan, where Ziliani was one of the first to hear it.

THE FINAL AUDITIONS: SICILIANI AND GAVAZZENI

Our youthful threesome was now, by force of cicrcumstance, beginning to move in separate directions. Mirella Freni was well on her way to the top, which she reached in 1963 at La Scala, with the acclaimed production of *Bohème* conducted by Von Karajan and directed by Zeffirelli. Pavarotti, meanwhile, was building his career in the manner we have seen.

I was troubled with neuroses and phobias, perhaps due to too many years of unremitting piano studies. For the time being I had stopped working as a pianist and conductor. I was now employed in less exhausting activities which were nonetheless still useful for my artistic development: chorus master, deputy singing master, and coach for leading singing groups.

From this point in my narrative, therefore, some episodes in Pavarotti's career are not written entirely from first-hand experience, though they were reported to me by people who can be trusted absolutely. The events I am about to relate were witnessed by Alessandro Ziliani and Francesco Siciliani.

Siciliani has been, without a shadow of doubt, one of the cleverest and most far-sighted men in the history of Italian theatre. His diplomatic skills and deep humanist culture were combined with musical sensibility and scholarship of the very first order.

During the years I spent with him as an Artistic Director at La Scala, I often saw him at the piano, sight-reading difficult and complicated orchestral scores such as Busoni's *Doktor Faust* and Debussy's *Pelléas et Mélisande*, always with a technical command that would have been the envy of many an orchestra conductor.

One day in the early Sixties, while we were having coffee at the Caffè Biffi, Siciliani asked me to join the artistic staff of this great Milanese theatre. I reluctantly declined because of prior engagements. We agreed to discuss it again another time. On that occasion he also asked me, casually, as if it were a trivial matter, what I thought of that young tenor from my home town who seemed fairly talented – yes, that Favarotti or Pacchierotti – the Maestro frowned in his rather crafty way, pretending not to remember the name.

I answered enthusiastically, praising his artistic and vocal qualities. As he listened, Siciliani seemed almost to be thinking about other things; all the same, I noticed that he was very interested in what I was saying.

Pavarotti was sunbathing on the banks of the Secchia, the river much loved by the people of Modena. (The people who live in the Bassa Modenese, the area comprising towns such as Bomporto, Ravarino, Finale Emilia and Massa Finalese, have closer ties with the Panaro, the other river that waters the soil of Emilia. But people from the city prefer the area between Marzaglia and Bruciata, where the Secchia flows, shaded by dense poplar woods, before tumbling into the Po a few dozen kilometres downstream.)

Luciano was relaxing after the pressures of *Rigoletto* in Piacenza. He was wearing shorts, a light T-shirt and a pair of comfortable clogs. He was enjoying deep lungfuls of the pure riverside air, when suddenly he saw his car, a Ford Cortina bought with his first theatre earnings, bumping towards him on the narrow unpaved track leading from Via Emilia to the banks of the Secchia. His young wife Adua climbed out and said excitedly, "Luciano, you must leave for Milan at once. Ziliani phoned. He wants you in his office by 4pm. You're not to lose a single minute. It's about something very important".

Luciano looked at the clock: it was almost midday; even if he drove at top speed it would take a miracle to reach Milan by four, given the chaos

Modena, 30 September 1961 – Luciano and Adua are married. The witness is Alessandro Ziliani.

of traffic clogging the Via Emilia. He decided to try anyway. He gave his wife the bicycle that was lying on the riverbank, and sat down at the steering wheel of the Ford, just as he was.

A few hours earlier, in Milan, Siciliani had heard that the stage of La Scala would be free that afternoon, because the lorry bringing the scenery for Spontini's *Olimpia* had been involved in an accident. He had instantly seized the opportunity to summon a few singers he was interested in, among them the up-and-coming tenor from Modena that Ziliani had spoken of with such enthusiasm several months ago.

At ten to four, drenched with sweat, and having risked his neck repeatedly, Luciano parked in a "No Parking" space in Via Santa Radegonda. Ziliani was waiting for him nervously at the office door; when he saw Luciano he almost had a fit.

"But Luciano, what a state you're in! In a few minutes we have to be at La Scala for an audition with Siciliani!"

Suddenly Luciano realised the absurdity of the situation. He tried to protest: "I was told to leave without a moment's delay. If I'd gone home to change I would have lost almost an hour…".

But Ziliani was hardly listening; he was rummaging frantically in his office wardrobe. Triumphantly he pulled out an impeccable blue suit. Luciano tried to get into it, but had to stop as soon as the trousers showed worrying signs of splitting. Desperate, the two of them decided to go to the theatre just as they were. They had a difficult time with La Scala's strict doormen, especially the unbending Bergamini, who had no intention of letting in that "beach bum" (as he described him to his colleagues), dressed in shorts and clogs. He kept repeating Ghiringhelli's ruling that anyone entering La Scala should be dressed in keeping with the dignity of the place. Explaining the situation to him required all Ziliani's patience and diplomatic skills.

Once they had finally reached the waiting room on the first floor, Luciano felt more at ease. The four or five others waiting their turn, all tenors, had other things on their mind. They gave him no more than a brief, scornful glance, preoccupied as they were with warming up their voices with the most extravagant assortment of vocal exercises.

Finally Pavarotti managed to concentrate on the pieces he was going to sing: the arias from *Bohème* and *Rigoletto*.

When Antonio Tonini, who was in charge of understudies at La Scala, accompanied him onto the stage, Luciano failed to respond to the subtle irony behind the question: "What are you going to sing? Pollione's aria from *Norma?*" (Pollione appears on stage bare-legged).

"No, Maestro: 'Che gelida manina'," he replied calmly.

He had regained his confidence, and was barely touched by the reverential fear that all singers experience the first time they tread the boards of that great theatre.

Siciliani was sitting half-way up the stalls, and for a moment he thought his eyes were deceiving him when he saw Luciano firmly planted in the middle of the stage. Ziliani was explaining to him the reasons for his protégé's strange attire, when the poignant beginning of Rodolfo's aria silenced them both. That enchanting voice was already working its magic, and the two old friends, moved by it, listened without saying another word.

Puccini's aria sufficed for Siciliani to realise that he was observing a remarkable singer. At the end of that round of auditions only Luciano was called to his office. The others were dismissed with elegant and honeyed words.

He offered Luciano a début at La Scala in either *I Puritani* or *Guglielmo Tell*. Pavarotti listened calmly and replied, very wisely, that he did not yet feel ready for those operas. He would be happy to perform his repertoire: *La bohème, Rigoletto, Traviata*.

"But for those we already have Di Stefano, Kraus, Raimondi, Bergonzi..." Siciliani replied, somewhat piqued. "I could only offer you the understudy roles, which wouldn't be quite enough for you. And you'd have to audition with Maestro Gavazzeni, who usually directs that repertoire..."

"Well, thank you Maestro," Luciano replied, "for the time being I shall continue with my career outside La Scala, then we'll see."

And the two men said goodbye to each other – cordially, but not too warmly.

In the meantime, Luciano's career beyond La Scala was advancing with ever greater success. 18th January 1963 saw his début in *Lucia di Lammermoor* in Holland, with Virginia Zeani in the lead role. The role of Edgardo was perfectly suited to his voice, which was becoming ever more luminous and harmonically rich, so much so that the famous invective "Hai tradito il cielo e amor" ("You have betrayed the heavens and love itself"), which Ziliani always described as a bugbear, was mastered with no difficulties at all. His growing repertoire now contained a fourth opera, which was to give him even greater satisfaction.

(© 1989, Judith Kovacs)

At the same time, he continued ceaselessly to perform *Bohème*, *Rigoletto* and *Traviata*, the three operas which helped to form his voice during his early career. On 24th February and 27th April 1963 he performed *Bohème* and *Rigoletto* at the Vienna Opera. This was his baptism on the international stage.

Luciano was unaware that in one of the boxes of the darkened theatre Maestro Herbert von Karajan was watching the performance. This distinguished Austrian, who discovered and launched so many new singers, was to give the decisive push that would lead to young Luciano's recognition.

Ziliani, meanwhile, was keen to approach La Scala again. Following Siciliani's advice, he asked Gavazzeni to audition Luciano. Maestro Gavazzeni, from Bergamo, generally conducted the repertoire Luciano preferred, and a role at La Scala depended on his approval.

By this time Luciano had sworn to stop doing auditions – those rather humiliating private displays that artists have to endure, of necessity, until they are well-established – or sometimes when they are ageing singers in decline. Given the quality and quantity of work he was being offered, he could allow himself this luxury.

Ziliani persuaded him to make an exception for Gavazzeni, as the stakes were so high. He agreed to undergo this unpleasant trial for the last time.

We set off together for Bergamo. Luciano drove in a rather daredevil way, but with skill and quick reflexes. (Soon afterwards he had a frightening road accident in Yugoslavia, which persuaded him to moderate his speed.) During the journey we discussed Gavazzeni. We both respected him as a highly cultured musician, sensitive both as a man and as an artist. We knew of his friendship with Di Stefano, and Luciano was not sure that the Maestro would like his use of "covered sounds" in the *passaggi* or changes of register. Gavazzeni welcomed us most amiably on the stage of the Teatro Donizetti. We had prepared three pieces – usually more than enough for auditions. Luciano began with "Che gelida manina", and since Gavazzeni, deep in thought in the darkness of the stalls, gave no sign of life, he continued with "Tombe degli avi miei".

He had rarely been asked to sing more than two arias, so, in view of the Maestro's continued silence, he hazarded, "Is that enough?".

"Carry on!" came the loud, authoritarian reply from the auditorium.

A little disconcerted, Luciano began the third aria, Massenet's "Ah, dispar vision", one of his favourites in those years. When he had finished, hearing no comment, we were about to leave, but another "Carry on!" stopped us in our tracks.

"Maestro, we have no more music," announced Luciano firmly.

Gavazzeni's white head slowly emerged from the darkness at the back of the stalls.

"I'm sorry, but I absolutely have to hear other pieces. Our music library is closed today, but I know that Magiera has a good memory. Can you let me hear Cavaradossi's two arias?"

I nodded to Luciano, who then sang "Recondita armonia" and "Lucean le stelle" in quick succession.

The five arias did not seem to have sapped his energy in the slightest; his voice was still as fresh and scintillating as it had been at the start of the audition. But Gavazzeni seemed determined to put him to the test; unperturbed, he then asked for the three arias from *Rigoletto*.

"We'll do those as well," muttered Luciano, "but that's all."

He was starting to sweat, with good reason; opera arias require great effort of concentration and breath control, and eight arias in a row are no mean exploit.

Nevertheless, he sang them perfectly, firing off a B natural at the end of "La donna è mobile" that in our opinion should have satisfied the most demanding listener. But Gavazzeni was not taking anything for granted.

"Now I would like to hear 'Quanto è bella, quanto è cara', and 'Una furtiva lacrima'."

"Maestro, could I at least have a glass of water?" asked Luciano, somewhat ironically.

"I'm sorry, but today there are no performances, and we have no serving staff. Anyway, young man, at your age you don't need water in order to sing a few songs."

"Whatever you say, Maestro," was Luciano's faintly rebellious reply, before the two arias from *Elisir d'amore* brought his total to ten.

I was also beginning to tire a little: all those pieces required immense concentration to play from memory, and I suddenly realised I was bathed in sweat from head to toe. We were hoping with all our hearts that our tyrant had had enough.

Imperiously, Gavazzeni announced: "Good, now the two arias from *Favorita* should be enough for me, and maybe 'A te o cara' from *Puritani*; but if you don't remember 'Una vergin, un angiol di Dio,' then 'Spirto gentil' will do," said Gavazzeni sweetly in answer to Luciano's objection.

Maybe the two final arias did not quite reach such towering heights as the other ten, or perhaps, as we had feared, some "covered sound" was not to the liking of this renowned and most exacting conductor. The fact remains that Gavazzeni, at the end of this tour de force, dismissed Luciano with a few formal compliments, telling him, essentially, that he did not think he was good enough yet to sing at La Scala under his baton.

AT LAST LA SCALA

Gavazzeni's spectacular rejection was probably fortunate for Luciano. He carried on putting in time (he used a much more vivid anatomical term) often in highly prestigious theatres, though none so dangerous as La Scala.

On 7th May 1963, in Belfast, he added a fifth opera to his repertoire: *Madama Butterfly*. Later, he gradually abandoned Pinkerton for the same reason that he gave up Alfredo in *Traviata* – the male role was overshadowed by the female.

I should add that if Pavarotti felt any regrets about giving up the role of Alfredo, the same cannot be said about Pinkerton, a role he never much liked because of the character's male chauvinist egoism. Furthermore, Pinkerton was behind one of the rare disappointments of his career: he recorded *Madama Butterfly* with Mirella Freni and Herbert von Karajan, but in the subsequent film with the same cast, he was replaced by his arch-rival Placido Domingo, for aesthetic and cinematographic reasons.

Two months later, on 24th July 1964, came a valuable and formative experience, one that has perhaps not been fully appreciated by his biographers up to now: his Mozart début. He made no less than seventeen appearances as Idamante, Idomeneo's son, twelve at Glyndebourne and five at the Grand Théâtre in Geneva.

Luciano had often attempted Mozart's Italian arias, particularly those sung by Don Ottavio in *Don Giovanni*: "Dalla sua pace" and "Il mio tesoro intanto", but also "Un'aura amorosa" from *Così fan tutte*.

My views on the usefulness of Mozart's music for improving vocal technique can be found in technical appendix no. 6. In the meantime I would stress that his experience at Glyndebourne, which at that time was probably the festival that paid the most attention to the artistic preparation of the choruses, left an indelible mark on Pavarotti's personality.

Jani Strasser knew how to instil an iron discipline into the singers who received her rigid, scientifically-based instruction. From her Luciano also learned the rules of professionalism that characterised all the artists who took their turn on the Glyndebourne stage at that time: Sesto Bruscantini, Geraint Evans, Luis Alva, Giuseppe Modesti, Juan Oncina, Tatiana Menotti, Teresa Berganza, Ilva Ligabue, Mirella Freni, Joan Sutherland and others.

Through *Idomeneo* at Glyndebourne, Pavarotti experienced an international ambience that was stimulating and rich in ideas, where one could have illuminating discussions during informal encounters in the bar of the great country house, with artists such as Vittorio Gui, Colin Davis, John Pritchard, Carl Ebert, Gunther Rennert, and Franco Enriquez.

Among the group of singers, too, there was a companionship rarely to be found elsewhere, made possible by prolonged periods of rehearsal and sustained concentration on the work. Besides, there were few distractions in that rain-soaked English village. The only diversion allowed was a Saturday outing to Brighton.

The continual exchange of ideas was culturally enriching for all, and the younger singers, such as Mirella and Luciano, benefited particularly from this.

Many years later, at the Metropolitan in New York in 1982, and again at the Salzburg Festival in 1983, I heard Pavarotti as Idomeneo rather than Idamante. It had become traditional to perform the role of King of Crete in a rather bloodless way. In Pavarotti's Idomeneo, characterised by a wealth of vocal expression, I recognised yet more of the teachings of the "Glyndebourne school".

In contrast with an established German tradition, Jani Strasser believed that Mozart should be performed with as much richness of colour, tone, and even vocal power as any other type of music, and this applied even to those stylistic aspects which I discuss later in this book. She maintained that the flatness and tedium resulting from an excess of "style" would betray the vitality and openness of Mozart's music, which prefigures so many romantic and even modern developments in music.

Because Pavarotti's Idomeneo reflected these ideas, he was inevitably attacked by the more conservative critics. However, he earned the unconditional approval of the public as well as the respect of musicians such as Karajan, Gavazzeni and Jean-Pierre Ponnelle. I heard them discussing his performance and agreeing unanimously that it was the best they had ever seen.

I return now to 1964 – a magical year in Luciano's career. By this time his longed-for début at La Scala was imminent: the great opera house in Milan could no longer ignore the young tenor who was winning praise right round the world.

He was invited to take part in La Scala's first tour to Moscow, only "on the bench as a sub" (I use the metaphor advisedly; football was one of Pavarotti's favourite sports in his youth). He was ready to go on in

Bohème directed by von Karajan, if Gianni Raimondi's sore throat should worsen in the freezing Russian climate.

Mirella Freni was in Moscow too, and our little study group was revived. We worked intensively, partly because the bad weather often prevented us from leaving the hotel.

Luciano was preparing for other important débuts, including *Sonnambula*, *Elisir*, *Figlia del Reggimento*, and *Capuleti e Montecchi*, while Mirella was being tested to the limit in the difficult role of Violetta, often receiving advice from Karajan himself. As I got to know him more closely at last, I was astonished by Karajan's willingness to discuss problems of interpretation in Verdi's opera. He had immense charisma, and my hands would tremble a little whenever I played the piano in his presence. His knowledge of Italian opera was endless; he told me he had been Toscanini's assistant and, before that, Tullio Serafin's. In spite of this, he was rarely dogmatic, always prepared to reconsider an idea if he found Mirella's or my observations to be fair and well-founded.

We admired this eminent conductor all the more for his humility as an artist and his thirst for perfection. We already knew he had played a part in Luciano's selection for La Scala's team.

When, on 26th September 1964, Pavarotti gave a concert on Moscow television, Karajan made a special point of remarking favourably on the young man who had so impressed him in Vienna.

During the following months, besides his many routine appearances, Pavarotti performed with Joan Sutherland in *Lucia di Lammermoor* in Miami and Fort Lauderdale. From then on she took him under her wing.

Towards the end of April 1965, the bizarre spring weather in Milan led to another bout of tonsillitis for Gianni Raimondi, forcing him to cancel his performance on the 28th. Panic ensued among the management at La Scala over the difficult choice of his replacement. There were more than a few proponents of Giacomo Aragall, another young man who was making a name for himself at the time. But Karajan was adamant: only Pavarotti was good enough to go on stage as Rodolfo, under his baton, without any rehearsals.

Judging from leaked information from the summit meeting in the Yellow Room, it seems that Siciliani favoured the Aragall solution. To be fair to Siciliani it has to be said that the Spaniard was at that time a formidable rival to Pavarotti. If, later on, he had made better use of the splendid gifts he was born with, he could surely have been among the three or four greatest tenors in the world.

Miami, February 1965 - With Joan Sutherland in Lucia di Lammermoor.
(Photo Pineda)

But Karajan's determination silenced even Siciliani. There were only a few days to go before the début, and Karajan personally asked me to check over the music for *La bohème* with Pavarotti. I found Luciano a little discouraged; his doctor had just diagnosed some inflammation of the vocal cords, and had prescribed five days of absolute voice rest – five days before his first, most important appearance at La Scala.

We both decided not to do the music revision Karajan had requested.

Milan, 1966 - Piazza della Scala. (© Publifoto)

Instead, Luciano became absolutely mute, as the doctor had advised. He communicated with his family by writing messages, and only once did he answer the telephone, when the costume department wanted to know his measurements. He did not wish to arouse any suspicions about his state of health.

Finally the big day arrived; I was as nervous as I had been on the day of his début in *La bohème* in Reggio Emilia. Luciano, on the other hand, seemed calm, but perhaps this apparent calmness was due to his continuing silence. Showing amazing *sang-froid*, he even chose not to warm up before the performance – so as to spare his vocal cords as much as possible.

I stayed with him in the wings right up to the moment he was to go on stage. He looked slightly pale. Finally, a second before going on, he opened his mouth and said just two words: "Ho paura" ("I'm scared").

As soon as he set foot on the stage he was transformed. He was immediately in the role, and his voice, strengthened by the days of total rest, rang out as easily as ever.

I saw Karajan give him a satisfied smile from the podium after the first splendid B flat ("Aguzza l'ingegno. L'idea avvampi in fiamma") and I, too, finally managed to calm down.

After "Che gelida manina" the whole theatre burst into wild and prolonged applause. Even Karajan put down his baton and joined in.

THE GOLDEN YEARS

Two days after his début at La Scala, having been checked by the throat specialist and given the all-clear, Luciano came to my house carrying two scores: *La sonnambula* and *L'elisir d'amore*.

Joan Sutherland, who has been one of the major influences on his technical development, had persuaded him to tackle a hitherto unexplored vocal style. I call it *bel canto*, referring to Bellini and Donizetti, but some of the more precious Italian critics insist on calling it post-*bel canto*, because they consider the term *bel canto* applicable only to the baroque repertoire.

I have already said a little about the Mozartian style. *Bel canto* is something of a middle way between Mozart and Verdi. From Mozart it uses the technique of singing high up in the "mask", only softer and more cantabile; and it anticipates Verdi in some ways through its sense of the *legato*, and its long, expressive phrases. But there is a difficulty with these melodies, so smooth and flowing and so enchantingly "singable", (consider "A te o cara" from *I Puritani*). The difficulty lies in their sudden bursts into the top register, which pose serious problems for singers who lack a complete command of the very highest notes.

This is the difficulty with the stretta "Tutto, ah tutto in quest'istante" in the first act of *Sonnambula*; many tenors of the past would avoid it by removing the high Cs.

Naturally Luciano would not hear of any such easy solutions. Nonetheless, even though he was gifted with exceptional vocal range, those phrases caused him more than a little consternation.

His voice was not yet accustomed to this style of singing, and it tended to be a little too heroic, without the lightness needed to climb effortlessly up that murderous vocal *tessitura*. It is possible that Bellini still had in mind the timbre of the castrato voice when he composed this passage.

In a matter of weeks things improved markedly, and Luciano felt confident when he set off on a tour of Britain and Australia lasting several months.

He did not give me a date for his return, but appeared at my house in his usual way, without knocking, to find me preparing the English baritone Peter Glossop for his début in *Rigoletto* at La Scala. Luciano was also in this production, and it was the first time his name had officially appeared on La Scala's posters. The news had caused an uproar in the Galleria and the meeting-places of Milanese music buffs. They were astonished by the preference accorded to Pavarotti at the expense of illustrious colleagues such as Gianni Raimondi, Giuseppe Di Stefano, Alfredo Kraus and Carlo Bergonzi.

Glossop, who was going full tilt at the monologue from the last act of *Rigoletto*, where the poor buffoon believes he has trodden on the corpse of the Duke of Mantova. He barely noticed the new arrival.

Luciano put a finger to his lips, not wanting me to interrupt the rehearsal. He sat on the sofa, absorbed in this gigantic British singer's beautiful rendering. A few bars before the Duke throws poor Rigoletto into consternation by intoning from backstage "La donna è mobile", I saw Luciano, out of the corner of my eye, creep out of the studio. Right after Glossop's mighty F sharp in "All'onda, all'onda", we heard Luciano's "La donna è mobile" echo from afar, with perfect timing. Astonished by the unexpected and realistic sound effects, Glossop stopped singing, and I took the opportunity to introduce them to each other.

After that they often studied together. The performance on 9th December was a huge success for them both, as well as for Margherita Rinaldi as Gilda, and the conductor Molinari Pradelli.

Rather than dwell on the subject of his début in *Rigoletto* at La Scala, I want to go back to that day in my studio in Modena.

As soon as Glossop left, Luciano gave me a detailed account of his Australian tour. After hearing him sing those few lines from the fourth act of Rigoletto, I was under the impression that his voice had improved recently, and I told him so.

"That's because of Sutherland," he explained, full of enthusiasm. "She's a wonderful colleague. She's persuaded me to reconsider my ideas on breathing."

Indeed, the length of his breaths, already perfectly respectable, had increased considerably. I was amazed when he sang Elvino's line, "Tutto, ah tutto in quest'istante" (containing those fearsome Cs,) in order to convince me of the validity of his new breathing method. I had never before heard from him such ease of vocal production, such beauty in the legatos, nor such brilliance in the high notes. I am the only person in Italy to have had the privilege of hearing his Elvino. On impulse, and to show me the progress he had made, he sang the entire part.

Unfortunately *Sonnambula* passed through his repertoire like a meteor. After his tour with Sutherland he never performed it again, leaving me

Melbourne, July/August 1965 – L'elisir d'amore. *(© The Herald & Weekly Times Ltd)*

with the memory of that fantastic, unrepeatable exhibition, which was mine alone.

Whenever I remembered how much light and energy were unleashed by his versions of *Traviata*, *Sonnambula*, and *Butterfly*, I was always saddened that he decided to drop these operas from his repertoire.

The great progress he had made as a result of observing, studying and singing with Sutherland also brought much-needed improvements to the production of *Rigoletto* at La Scala.

In this temple of opera, the groups and factions that support the various singers always look uncharitably on new talent, fearing the threat it poses. But in the case of a young person who is indisputably gifted (which was certainly true of Pavarotti), even the fiercest partisans are reduced to silence.

In the course of Luciano's many performances, no-one lamented the absence of Gianni Raimondi, hitherto unequalled as the Duke of Mantova. The Milanese idol Giuseppe di Stefano was missed still less; long ago, in a performance of *Rigoletto*, he had weathered a stormy night of whistles aimed in equal measure at him and his illustrious colleagues Ettore Bastianini and Rosanna Carteri.

It is customary for young singers to include in their *curriculum vitae* the names of eminent conductors they have worked with. Let us now take a look at those who conducted Pavarotti in his early years at La Scala.

After *La bohème* with Karajan, Luciano found himself reunited with Molinari Pradelli. He was one of the most graceful conductors I ever saw; his harmonious and powerful gestures seemed to combine the precise geometry of a fencer with the fearless unruliness of a sabre-fighter. Unfortunately his tongue was also as quick and sharp as the blade of a sword. In the sophisticated environment of La Scala his attacks would inevitably rebound on him, and he was banished from the theatre for long periods. His severity towards singers was somewhat suspect too; it may well have stemmed from feelings of jealousy, for he would seem vexed and ill-tempered whenever the audience showed particular appreciation for an artist's vocal prowess.

His relationship with Luciano was always slightly ambiguous, and once, in Bologna, it flared into a blazing row. During rehearsals in Milan, their relationship was marked by a cold and detached formality.

The many performances of *La bohème* that Pavarotti took over from Raimondi were conducted by Nino Sanzogno. This aristocratic Venetian also possessed enviable elegance as a conductor, and his renowned fluency in reading scores had made him one of the top specialists in contemporary music.

His rather detached nature did not always allow him to do justice to Grand Opera, however. In *Carmen* and *Elisir d'amore*, for instance, Sanzogno found himself facing a barrage of whistles. He would respond with a sardonic, imperturbable smile, at the same time mouthing "Sons of bitches" almost imperceptibly, repeating the phrase like a prayer until the storm was over.

I have already mentioned Gianandrea Gavazzeni, and will do so again. Meanwhile, the record shows that the other eminent conductor at La Scala during those years, Antonino Votto, never conducted Pavarotti, partly because of a curious set of circumstances, partly because of the difference in their ages.

Amongst the conductors too there was a feeling that a breath of fresh air was needed. It was Luciano who brought a great new talent into the fold: Claudio Abbado.

I had enjoyed meeting Abbado a few years earlier, at the finals of a piano competition in which we both took part. I watched his first rehearsals at La Scala with great interest. The orchestra were not entirely confident of him at first, but they soon began to trust him, becoming increasingly enthralled by this gifted young man with his prodigious memory. His gestures were commanding and brilliantly effective, and he knew how to galvanise the musicians, fanning the flames of romance in Bellini's *I Capuleti e i Montecchi*.

This was the ninth opera in Pavarotti's repertoire, and the production was hugely successful. It was recorded, and went on tour to Rome, Holland, Edinburgh and Canada.

Abbado's conducting proved fresh, original and extremely concise. The singers provided an unforgettable display of *bel canto*. Renata Scotto gave one of the best performances of her life, and the duet between Aragall (Romeo) and Pavarotti (Tebaldo) was sensational, enhanced by the rivalry between the two most promising young tenors on the international scene at the time.

After this golden moment, he mastered his tenth opera, *La figlia del Reggimento*, or rather, *La fille du Régiment*, which Donizetti originally composed in French, but rewrote in Italian immediately afterwards.

Since it was now becoming fashionable to sing opera in the original language, the very Italian *Figlia* became *La fille* in the performance staged by Covent Garden on 2nd June 1966. In actual fact, quite apart from the scholarly justification, there was also the need to please the divine Sutherland, who was much more at ease with French than with Italian.

Even Pavarotti agreed, for the first time, to sing an opera in a language other than Italian. He was anxious not to displease his powerful friend, to whom he felt close ties of gratitude and affection.

His French turned out to be rather awkward, a fact which did not escape comment by some of the more malicious London critics, but his singing reached such heights that he even outshone Sutherland, who was loved and admired in the Anglo-Saxon world even more than Maria Callas was in Italy.

It was a complete novelty in the world of opera to hear the *bel canto* repertoire, until then the domain of "light" or "light-lyric" tenors, sung by a full-lyric voice such as Luciano's. No one before him had been able to sing *legato* with such absorbing warmth of expression yet also reach those nine famous Cs with exhilarating power. The accolade of the Covent Garden audience was such that, at the end of the cabaletta, the performance literally had to stop for twenty minutes.

In spite of his immense acclaim Pavarotti retained close ties with his roots – with the theatres and friends of his birthplace. He was a frequent guest of the operatic societies that exist in every small town in Emilia. These groups of opera-lovers were his first real fans. Yet the managers of his "own" theatre had been remarkably slow to realise the great artistic stature of their fellow citizen.

It was not until 1966 that Luciano went on tour with Modena's Teatro Comunale, all past misunderstandings generously forgotten. In Yugoslavia, at the Narodne Pozoziste theatre in Sarajevo, our company had an outstanding success with *Bohème*; I was conducting, with Freni and Pavarotti together on stage.

This had come about after Luciano had starred in a memorable *Rigoletto* in Rome and Florence, directed by Eduardo de Filippo and conducted by Carlo Maria Giulini in one of his last operatic appearances. Modena at last welcomed Luciano with open arms, eager to celebrate his huge success.

Modena staged Luciano's first Italian performance of *Elisir d'amore*, with Gianfranco Masini conducting. As Nemorino, he delighted the Modenese audience, who were almost dismayed to rediscover on their own doorstep this vocal phenomenon who moved with utter simplicity from the first quasi-baritone resonances of "Quant'è bella, quant'è cara"

Milan, La Scala Opera Season 1965/66: Rigoletto – *With director Margherita Wallmann. (© E. Piccagliani)*

Milan, La Scala Opera Season 1968: I Capuleti e i Montecchi – *With the tenor Giacomo Aragall (Claudio Abbado's début at La Scala). (© E. Piccagliani)*

to the thrilling agility of the duets with Adina, Dulcamara and Belcore, releasing high notes of indescribable beauty before reaching the final masterpiece "Furtiva lacrima", the *pièce de résistance* of all great tenors of the past.

In the total silence of a packed theatre his amazing *legato*, his singing taut as the sweep of a great cellist's bow, overshadowed memories of even the greatest performances of the past. Perhaps only Caruso had possessed such a combination of mysterious resonances, such a potent splendour of harmonic sounds.

I cannot remember a more triumphant accolade than the one bestowed on Luciano after that aria. It began to look as if the curtain would have to come down before the end of the opera; and only after several attempts was Masini able to reach the end.

11th November 1967 marked the beginning of Luciano's great conquest of America. He had previously sung in Miami and Fort Lauderdale, but he had then been in the retinue of "Her Majesty" Joan Sutherland, and those cities were not on the grand American theatre circuit.

His engagement in San Francisco followed his successes at La Scala and Covent Garden. The Californian opera house was, with good reason, one of the three top American venues, together with the Metropolitan in New York and the Lyric Opera of Chicago.

He appeared in his favourite opera, *Bohème*, with Mirella Freni in the lead female role. It was an enormous success. He received offers from all over the USA, and decided rightly to accept the Metropolitan's, where his début took place the following year.

Meanwhile, his own city wanted him back; the frenzied populace demanded his presence after the years of absence imposed by the short-sighted management of the Teatro Comunale. And so we did *Bohème* again, featuring Freni and me, in the production that had been such a hit in Sarajevo.

Immediately after that came another important performance: *La figlia del Reggimento*, finally in Italian, at La Scala.

The few days leading up to the rehearsals were nerve-racking for us because Mirella, who was to sing the daunting role of the *vivandière* Maria for the first time, had developed a worrying problem with her voice. It is possible she had not yet fully recovered psychologically from her fall during *Traviata* at La Scala a few years earlier. On top of this, she had been suffering for some time with an intestinal condition that made it difficult for her to breathe deeply, which of course all singers have to do. Whatever the reasons, the high register was not responding with its usual strength and clarity, and she was deeply worried about this difficult début in an opera full of long, perilous high notes.

We decided to hold a meeting and examine the problem thoroughly. With his usual generosity, Luciano cancelled a number of concerts, I did the same with mine, and for about two weeks we devoted ourselves to resolving Mirella's problem, requesting a later starting date for rehearsals at La Scala.

With great patience Luciano persuaded her to adopt the breathing technique Sutherland had taught him. By demonstration, often singing the soprano part too, he helped her to regain full control of her abdominal muscles, grown slack and weak from her long illness. The results were swift. Mirella soon began to trill with the agility of a light soprano, and reached notes that had previously been beyond her, such as high D and high E flat.

The "Sutherland cure" had worked miracles for her too. At the first rehearsal in the theatre, Maestro Sanzogno's irritation at their late start soon gave way to his customary Venetian good humour as he saw how perfectly prepared the two singers were.

On the opening night, 26th February 1968, the audience's rapture knew no limits. No one at La Scala could remember anything to rival Pavarotti's virtuosity in the aria with the nine Cs. Freni, too, triumphed in every respect: her faultless agility, her high notes, and the magnificent legato of "Convien partir". It was a memorable victory, not only over her own demons, but also over her opponents at La Scala.

NEW CONQUESTS

Luciano was now in superb vocal shape, with seven years of a very intensive career behind him. He felt the time had come to test his strength in one of the two operas considered to be the ultimate goals for a tenor: *I Puritani* and *Guglielmo Tell*.

He chose first of these, which is more "belcantistic" although also higher than the second. And he chose the Teatro Massimo Bellini in Catania, where the atmosphere is not as torrid as in some northern Italian theatres, and where a false note from a singer does not send local councils and mayors into a spin.

The conductor was Argeo Quadri who, although perhaps a little sidelined by the Italian establishment, was nonetheless an extremely competent musician, well versed in the opera tradition.

The other singers were distinguished too: Gabriella Tucci, Aldo Protti and the very young Ruggero Raimondi, who had also been a pupil of mine.

On 22nd March 1968, singing the entire opera in its original key, Pavarotti added his name to the very short list of performers who had survived, unharmed, the tremendous difficulties posed by the role of Arturo. In the previous fifty years only Giacomo Lauri Volpi, Mario Filippeschi, Gianni Raimondi and Alfredo Kraus are worth remembering, and at least two of these (Lauri Volpi and Raimondi) would often lower "A te o cara" by a semi-tone.

The exuberant Sicilian audience went wild over that voice, so dazzling and accurate in all the most difficult moments – those C sharps and D naturals that the opera is filled with.

One spectator in particular, a certain Millici, who was a well-known figure in the community, took to following Pavarotti to every theatre and shouting out a colourful phrase in Sicilian dialect, "*È Bellini ca ti manna*" ("You've been sent by Bellini"), after each song or bravura passage. He was often scolded and sometimes even removed from the theatre for his frenzied, fiery expressions of enthusiasm.

Now with the satisfaction of having climbed the tenors' "Everest", and with eleven operas in his repertory, Pavarotti continued with numerous performances of his usual *Bohème*, *Lucia*, *Traviata*, and others.

Meanwhile, in New York, fans at the Met were struggling to get hold of

Milan, La Scala Opera Season 1965/66: La bohème – *With Mirella Freni.*
(© E. Piccagliani)

tickets for the production of *La bohème* from Milan with Nino Sanzogno on the podium, Mirella Freni, and above all that long awaited young tenor who had caused such a sensation in San Francisco.

The first performance was a triumph, as expected; but the second was marked by a minor drama: after the first act, Pavarotti suddenly fell ill with tracheitis, and had to withdraw. The Metropolitan had to wait almost two years for his return. By now all the opera houses in the world were competing for him and his schedule had become frenetic.

In 1969, among other things, he performed *Puritani* again, in a production by the Teatro Comunale in Bologna, which also saw Mirella Freni's splendid début in the role of Elvira. On 31st May 1969 he made his twelfth opera début, as Des Grieux in Massenet's *Manon* at La Scala, once again with Freni.

The lead-up to this production was fraught with controversy. Initially, Georges Prêtre, the eminent French conductor, had been invited to the podium. He was convinced that he would be conducting the original French version, while Pavarotti and Freni believed they would be singing in Italian. This incredible and bizarre misunderstanding lasted until a few days before the start of rehearsals. When Prêtre realised he could not persuade the two stars to sing in French, he announced his withdrawal, firing off complaints about the mental laziness of Italian singers in general, and of Freni and Pavarotti in particular. These two were, of course, utterly blameless, since no-one at La Scala had informed them of Prêtre's wishes, and in any case it would have been impossible for them to study the French version at such short notice.

It has to be said that the audience at La Scala had no regrets about the Italian version; and the production was praised unreservedly.

20th November 1969 saw his thirteenth début, in another Verdi opera, *I Lombardi alla prima Crociata*, at the Opera in Rome, with Gianandrea Gavazzeni conducting.

By this time the two men were fully reconciled after the maestro from Bergamo had graciously admitted his error of judgement in that futile marathon of an audition a few years earlier. In fact they gradually established a mutual esteem, respect, and even friendship that lasted until Gavazzeni's death.

As with *Traviata*, *Butterfly* and *Sonnambula*, Luciano put *I Lombardi* on his reserve list, performing it very rarely. Only Oronte's famous aria "La mia letizia infondere" remained firmly in his concert repertory.

In 1970 Mirella, Luciano and I were invited to the Bilbao and Oviedo

Festival, the most prestigious opera festival in Spain, to give a few performances of Massenet's *Manon*.

Mirella and Luciano, mindful of the misunderstanding with Prêtre, diligently resolved to study the opera in French, only to be informed that in Spain this was absolutely unthinkable; all operas were sung in Italian, which was much easier for Spaniards to understand.

The Spanish trip was not without its setbacks: in Oviedo, just after her B flat in the final duet of the first act, Freni fell fainting into the arms of her partner. From the podium, I caught a glimpse of this scene as the curtain was closing, and I thought for a moment that they were joking. But when the applause began and they failed to come out and take their bows, I rushed onto the stage.

Mirella was in terrible pain and could hardly speak. A doctor was called immediately; he diagnosed an attack of cystitis, a condition which, in the acute stage, causes searing pains. The performance was suspended, to the dismay of the audience. We spent the next few days by her bedside. Mirella's blood pressure had also dropped suddenly, and she was not regaining her strength.

The impresarios, Laura and Arturo Barosi, were worried. Freni was due to star in *Elisir d'amore* as well as *Manon*. Since there was no chance of finding a replacement of the required calibre, the festival looked set for a serious disappointment

They summoned an eminent physician – Doctor Fanjul. In spite of her illness, Mirella had not altogether lost her sense of humour, and joked about the doctor's surname which, pronounced in Spanish, sounded like "*Fancul*" – an Italian obscenity. In spite of his name, he turned out to be an excellent physician, and in a few days we all sighed with relief when Mirella declared herself ready to resume her performances.

Then the Mayor made a proposal in an attempt to salvage the performance of *Manon* that had been suspended after the first act. He asked us if we would consider performing the magnificent St. Sulpice scene, in other words the third act of *Manon*, immediately after the last performance of *Elisir*. By this stratagem the audience would not have to be reimbursed for the suspended performance, and the artists would be paid as normal.

We cast questioning glances at each other. Maybe we were thinking about the debts we had recently incurred: Mirella and I for the purchase of a splendid penthouse apartment in Via Giardini in Modena, and Luciano for a luxury villa in the same street; after a few moments we replied in unison, agreeing with the proposal.

The performance received wide coverage in the Iberian press, and took place before a packed and excited audience. Lengthy applause greeted Mirella's appearance. The entire city had been following the news about her illness with great trepidation, and Doctor Fanjul, a guest of honour that night, had his moment of glory for having restored her to health.

Pavarotti was in top form. There was such instinctive conviction and such impressive vocal gravity in his portrayal of Nemorino that he continually received ovations from the demanding audience.

In Spain, performances always begin late in the evening, so *Elisir* ended at about two in the morning. There was an hour-long interval to allow for the change of scenery and for the artists and audience to rest, then I raised my baton for the great St. Sulpice scene from *Manon*.

Luciano's transformation from ignorant peasant to scholarly preacher was perfect. Traditionally, French tenors have portrayed a Des Grieux full of romantic airs and affectations; Luciano's voice, on the other hand, effectively revealed the restlessness and vigour of the character. In the famous seduction scene, the emotional conviction of the acting was so intense that the audience were completely carried away.

It was four in the morning: the dressing room siege lasted until sunrise, then the exuberant Spanish crowd that gathered outside our windows at the Hotel Principado lulled us to sleep with folk-songs and dances.

15th October 1970 marked Pavarotti's return to the USA, in a hugely successful *Lucia* at the Metropolitan, with Scotto and Ruggero Raimondi. This was followed by his last ever performance in *Traviata*, which I suspect he agreed to do as a tribute to his great friend and teacher, Joan Sutherland.

In spite of his fame, Pavarotti still felt the need to maintain strong links with his home and friends from his youth. The records show a performance of *Lucia* at the Teatro Carani in Sassuolo, dedicated to the manager Roberto Costi, whose exceptional kindness and humanity are qualities rarely found in his profession.

The San Francisco Opera competed very consistently and intelligently with the Met for his services, offering him his fourteenth début, *Un ballo in maschera*, conducted by Mackerras, with Arroyo, Donath and Franco Bordoni, on 27th October 1971. This was a significant date for Pavarotti, eleven years after his début in *La bohème*. In that time his voice had acquired an extraordinary fullness, particularly in the middle and lower register, while preserving his facility with high notes almost intact.

Un ballo in maschera required a different approach to Verdi, more intense and dramatic than the light-operatic roles he had sung until then, such as Alfredo and the Duke of Mantova. He was able to adapt his singing spontaneously and naturally, and the result once again was a triumph.

It would be fair to say that up to that point, Pavarotti had not deviated at all from Ziliani's sensible career plan. He gave another performance of *Un ballo in maschera* on 22nd July 1972, his first appearance at the Arena in Verona, which for many years had been the uncontested kingdom of Del Monaco and Corelli, whose powerful voices were in their element in that vast amphitheatre.

Milan, La Scala Opera Season 1986/87: Un ballo in maschera. *(© Lelli & Masotti)*

Among the immense throng that filled the Arena on the opening night, there were the usual sceptics who doubted Pavarotti's ability to rise fully to the challenge of "Grand Verdian Opera". They were proved spectacularly wrong.

His voice sounded amplified, and his splendid vocal colour seemed to find concealed inner chambers of resonance in the arches and terraces of the Roman amphitheatre.

The most striking features of his performance were the amorous vitality that he poured into "La rivedrà nell'estasi" while retaining a sense of tragic, prescient melancholy; the second stanza of "Di' tu se fedele il flutto m'aspetta", wholly imbued with sorrowful *nostalgia*; the impassioned duet in the second act, and the outstanding delivery of the final scene.

And so in Italy too, the cunning and sophisticated home of melodrama, he was unanimously recognised as a true, great Verdian tenor.

7th December 1973 found him in San Francisco once again, for his fifteenth début, *La favorita*.

The role of Fernando is undoubtedly one of the most difficult roles in the entire tenor repertory. Dramatic outbursts alternate with romantic interludes, sweet melodies with stratospheric high notes. Until then it had been the preserve of the "*tenori lunghi*" who had tended to stick to a stereotyped portrayal of the character.

Pavarotti stormed into the role, bringing a new life and energy and sweeping away the dusty old conventions from the music. His high register was still intact, and he was again anointed "King of the High Cs," an exaggerated expression, but one that American audiences were fond of.

With Christmas approaching, it was time to return home. Besides, nearby, at the Teatro in Bologna, rehearsals were about to begin for his Italian début in *La favorita*.

OPERATIC DISPUTES

Christmas and New Year, in Italy as elsewhere, are a time of feasting, and Luciano indulged his love of food very freely that year. Home again with his wife and daughters, with the Christmas spirit all around and the company of so many friends and admirers, he threw himself into gastronomic exploits worthy of the best Modenese and Emilian traditions. By 2nd January 1974, the date of the dress rehearsal of *La favorita*, he had put on extra weight from too much home cooking after months of world-wide travel.

Dress rehearsals were not generally open to the public at that time, and Luciano was intending, unusually for him, to sing a little below par that day. He planned to sing some sections in *mezza voce* or at the lower octave, and others in the normal range. This is common practice among singers; its purpose is to spare the voice for optimum condition on the opening night.

But Pavarotti had not taken into account his immense popularity in Italy at that time. As the curtain rose, he found himself face to face with an unbelievably full Teatro Comunale. The creaking old boxes, capable of accommodating four or five people, had been besieged by dozens of noisy fans seemingly intent on defying the laws of physics.

Carlo Maria Badini and Piero Rattalino, who had recently managed to restore Bologna's Teatro Comunale to its former glory, had responded to the huge demand for tickets by opening the dress rehearsal to the public. It seems they had forgotten to inform the artists, who were compelled to sing the entire opera *a voce piena*, in full voice, so as not to disappoint the festive and enthusiastic crowd.

Drawing on his consummate experience, Luciano tried to emerge unscathed from "Una vergine, un angel di Dio", which requires the tenor to soar immediately to a high C sharp, without a warm-up.

It was clear, however, that his digestive system was making breathing a little difficult. But the dress rehearsal audience were not there to pick holes in the artists' performances; they greeted the aria and almost every phrase in it with frenetic applause. These continual interruptions began to annoy the stern and dogmatic Molinari Pradelli.

Traditionally, dress rehearsals take place in complete silence, and each interval saw Molinari Pradelli increasingly angry. By the interval before the fourth act he had become extremely tense and irritable, and he scornfully compared the audience's fond excesses to those of the Roman circus.

The long-anticipated moment came for the aria "Spirto gentil". With his breathing almost fully restored now, Pavarotti displayed his wonderful gifts: a textbook legato, an exceptional mastery of breath control, a high C that drove the audience into a frenzy.

In the 1970s numerous clubs and supporters groups with titles like "Friends of the Opera" were formed, their members prone to extravagant and deafening ecstasies. Luciano's prowess on the C sparked off a tumultuous contest between these worshippers of *bel canto*. The deputation from the Opera Club of Rovereto sul Secchia, several hundred strong and led by Fausto Ferrari, made an infernal din. Other clubs from Modena, Sassuolo, Parma and Nonantola were equally vociferous. The contingent from the newly-formed Luciano Pavarotti Club of Carpi, probably the first to adopt his name, abandoned their seats and, led by their president, Gianni Carretti, gathered en masse at the balustrade of the orchestra pit, in order to make their cries more audible. Jostling with members of other clubs trying to do the same thing, they risked breaking the old wooden rail between the stalls and the orchestra pit, causing much concern among the musicians.

The mob breathing down his neck and yelling in his ears forced Molinari Pradelli to interrupt the rehearsal for several minutes. By this time his nerves were in tatters. When he finally struck up again, he increased the tempo more and more, either to spite the audience or possibly Pavarotti himself, who was guilty of nothing more than provoking unbridled enthusiasm. His baton soon reached such a dizzying speed that the singers were in serious difficulty.

It was hard enough for Bruna Baglioni to keep up, but by the time they came to the tenor phrase "Vieni meco io m'abbandono", the speed was effectively at Formula One level.

Pavarotti realised the situation was getting out of hand. He slowed down his tempo, hoping that the orchestra would follow. But the conductor took no account of the singer's needs, and kept increasing the tempo until Luciano could no longer stay in time. He got behind, first by a quarter of a beat, then by half, until he was actually several beats behind the conductor, at which point he had to stop singing. Soon after, Molinari Pradelli broke off conducting, so as not to transform *La favorita* into a symphonic concert.

The audience watched in astonished, frozen silence as Pavarotti and

Pradelli briefly exchanged heated words, then raised their fists, their unequivocal gestures leaving no question as to how they intended to settle their differences once the rehearsal was over.

When the curtain fell, Molinari Pradelli, having perhaps reflected on the difference in weight between himself and his adversary, dashed from the podium and locked himself in his dressing room (the same dressing room, incidentally, in which fascists had once attacked Arturo Toscanini).

Despite Rattalino's anxious efforts to stop him, Pavarotti was just a few metres behind, unable for the second time that day to keep up with his nimble and fast-moving adversary. Reaching the fragile dressing room door, which he could easily have knocked down with a shoulder-barge, he suddenly stopped. Luciano was incapable of harming a fly, and all at once he saw the funny side of this absurd situation.

Molinari Pradelli, on the far side of the door, sounding positively hysterical, was repeating incessantly, "Time, time! You have to stay in time!".

Laughing, Luciano replied, "That's right, Maestro, and now it's time for dinner." And with that humorous remark the incident was closed.

FURTHER DÉBUTS

Fortunately, few theatrical quarrels last very long. Peace is usually re-established around a well-stocked table.

The incident between Pavarotti and Molinari Pradelli ended in wine and food, or more specifically Lambrusco and pigs' trotters, in a restaurant in Reggio Emilia cleverly chosen by Carlo Maria Badini – it was here that the two men had celebrated Luciano's début in *Bohème* in 1961. Their reconciliation made an enormous difference to the success of *Favorita* at the Teatro Comunale in Bologna, which also definitively confirmed the growing reputation of Renato Bruson.

Fortune did not smile on the production of *Favorita* at La Scala, which opened a few weeks later, on 28th January 1974. Despite its cast, which looked formidable on paper, it turned out to be an unexpected disaster. There is no doubt that audience attitude was partly to blame. When Shakespeare's "wind of madness" begins to blow in the upper gallery of La Scala, it can throw any cast or conductor into turmoil.

The hostilities began with the crowd showing displeasure with the fine and noble singer, Ivo Vinco. His wife, Fiorenza Cossotto, who had first been hailed a great singer while performing in this same opera at La Scala, and since then received huge acclaim everywhere she played this role, started to become nervous.

Cappuccilli, who was usually a pillar of strength in performance, was not on top form that evening, probably unsettled by the electric atmosphere. In the concertato, "Ah, che diss'egli" he made (if my memory serves) a simple but serious mistake, which broke the sequence of the canon, leading all the other singers into an irreparable series of badly-timed entries that transformed the grand finale into a medley of sounds more reminiscent of Schoenberg than of Donizetti.

There was an indescribable uproar from the gods: whistles and insults aimed at the almost certainly innocent conductor Nino Verchi, barks, howls and other unmentionable noises. It is not difficult to imagine how the singers must have felt.

There were still some hurdles remaining: Leonora's famous aria "O mio Fernando", and Pavarotti's "Spirto gentil". Cossotto sang the whole aria extremely well, and was coming to the end of the cabaletta in her usual self-possessed way. But who knows what devil possessed her to end on a B natural instead of the usual A. Although for a mezzo-soprano, B is extremely high, she was capable of singing even strong, firm C naturals.

But that evening was ill-fated: the note came out hesitant and wavering, and sparked off another furious uproar from the pitiless critics in the gods.

After all the other great singers had been savaged, one sacrificial lamb remained: Pavarotti, who had so quickly gained international fame and respect, and had managed to thrill the audience even on that difficult evening, with "Una vergine, un angel di Dio".

I called into his dressing room before the beginning of the last act. There was a general atmosphere of dismay backstage, but he alone remained enviably calm.

Shortly after, his "Spirto gentil" helped greatly to restore the balance of the evening's fortunes, and Cossotto, back on top form, sang the last duet perfectly. The final C of "È spenta" silenced the hecklers.

In 1974, after that terrible beginning, Pavarotti went on to win further acclaim from American, German and French audiences, beginning with his début in *Bohème* at the Paris Opera and the Sferisterio in Macerata.

(© 1989, Judith Kovacs)

At the end of the year he added a sixteenth opera, Verdi's *Luisa Miller*, to his repertory.

San Francisco won the bid for this big night: Pavarotti was more heroic, more "Verdian" than ever, and received interminable ovations after "Quando le sere al placido". Starring with him was a young soprano rapidly rising to fame – Katia Ricciarelli.

Another significant event was his début at the Salzburg Festival in 1975, in Karajan's *Bohème* with Freni.

On 12th September, he was back in his beloved San Francisco, in an exciting new *Trovatore*, with Joan Sutherland as Leonora. After fifteen years on the professional stage, Pavarotti now added the role of Manrico to his repertory. This had always been considered a role strictly for the lyric *spinto* tenor.

Like all new departures, the metamorphosis of a lyric tenor into a lyric *spinto* tenor always triggers lively debate among music-lovers and musicologists. The better-informed among them know that this is accomplished over time, letting nature take its course, and without any forcing of the voice. Others, less expert and therefore less inclined to accept innovation, criticise the singer's presumptuousness, predict a premature end to his career, and foretell all kinds of damage to his vocal apparatus.

With a few decades of hindsight, it seems fair to say that the predictors of doom were totally wrong. Pavarotti continued to add lyric *spinto* tenor roles to his repertory; his technique never wavered, and his voice showed not the slightest ill-effects from performing Verdi's more dramatic works.

The proof of this is that he was able to keep *Elisir d'amore* in his repertory, frequently alternating it with *Trovatore* in a short space of time: an achievement that very few tenors can claim, in the entire history of opera. To my knowledge, only Enrico Caruso, Carlo Bergonzi and occasionally Beniamino Gigli could alternate between these two disparate operas with the same nonchalance. In the eclecticism of his repertory Pavarotti went even further than those legendary figures, by giving ten performances of *I Puritani* with Sutherland at the Metropolitan in February 1976, shortly after *Trovatore* in San Francisco.

Pavarotti's vocal versatility was truly exceptional: I cannot recall any other tenor going from *Elisir d'amore* to *Trovatore*, and then to the stratospheric *tessitura* of *I Puritani* in the space of a few months.

On 8th March 1976 he made his eighteenth début, in Strauss's *Der*

Rosenkavalier, playing the minor but extremely challenging role of the Italian tenor. Only the Metropolitan and a handful of other theatres can permit themselves such luxury and refinement in their casting.

On 26th November 1976 he appeared in another new role, this time at the Lyric Opera in Chicago, home of the great Bruno Bartoletti. By now the entire music world was watching the famous tenor's every move with interest. The new role was Mario Cavaradossi, in Puccini's *Tosca*. This was a role Pavarotti had always refused when he was younger, as he felt that it was not yet suited to his developing voice.

Pavarotti had always loved *Tosca*, and his long and patient wait proved worthwhile, for the result was stunningly successful. By now his voice possessed the full palette of musical colours, which enhanced the character of Cavaradossi with amazing *chiaroscuri* and interpretative nuances.

Every opera house wanted to applaud his new roles. A production of *Tosca* in London followed, with Kabaivanska, splendid and regal as ever in the title role; then *Trovatore* in Vienna, with Karajan and a legendary cast (Leontyne Price, Christa Ludwig, Cappuccilli, Van Damm), *Der Rosenkavalier* in Hamburg, and many more.

In 1977 he continued his tradition of late autumn débuts with Puccini's

Milan, La Scala Opera Season 1979/80: Tosca. *(© Lelli & Masotti)*

Turandot at the War Memorial Opera House in San Francisco, where so many of his new roles were born. Pavarotti appeared as Calaf, alongside Caballé, Mitchell and a rising star, the conductor Riccardo Chailly. Although the performance was a great success, he never sang the part again. Perhaps he felt it was too heroic for his voice, in which there was always an element of gentleness and expressive pathos. Or perhaps he was not particularly keen on the music of Franco Alfano, who composed the final duet. For whatever reason, *Turandot* was added to the other operas he had shelved: *Sonnambula, Traviata, Butterfly, I Lombardi,* and *Capuleti e Montecchi*.

Even *La Gioconda*, which he first sang in San Francisco on 7th September 1979, was repeated only at the Arena in Verona. The role of Enzo Grimaldo (his twenty-first) fitted Luciano's voice perfectly, and he did in fact quite like singing it. His few appearances in it are due more to the fact that this is a difficult opera to stage. To those that saw them those performances were unforgettable, for the beauty of his sound and the enormous vigour he brought to Ponchielli's slightly dated melodies.

In his private life at about that time an unpleasant episode occurred, which upset his long-standing friendship with Renata Scotto and her husband, Lorenzo Anselmi. The story, involving a series of anonymous letters, is ugly and complicated, and not worth dwelling on. Yet it seriously damaged their working relationship, as well as their friendship and mutual respect, which went back to 1964, when they had first performed together in *Bohème* at the Teatro Sociale in Mantova.

In 1980, after twenty years on the stage, Pavarotti's voice was still as fresh and young as ever. His immense popularity, particularly in America, was both unprecedented and unrivalled by his contemporaries. His intelligent use of modern mass-media played a huge part in making his name widely known, as did the help he received from Herbert Breslin, the American agent who took care of his interests after Ziliani's premature death.

The public loved Pavarotti for his geniality, but above all for his artistic power which, though meditated and hard-earned, had a spontaneity and immediacy which went directly to the heart and soul of the listener.

Every Autumn Pavarotti's American audiences looked forward with enormous excitement to his début in a new opera. Once again San Francisco beat the others to the post, and was able to offer its subscribers Pavarotti's latest role: Radames. Margaret and Leontyne Price took turns in the role of *Aida* for the six performances, which were judged an "awesome" success, to use the Anglo-Saxon term.

A few months later, in 1981, at the Deutsche Oper in Berlin, I had a chance to hear Luciano's *Aida*. It is hard to find the words to describe the technical assurance, the fluency, the power of both sound and interpretation in his performance.

In 1981 Pavarotti fulfilled his old dream of singing the title role in Mozart's *Idomeneo*. After his Mozart experience, he presented another new role, his last, in the Autumn of 1983. The opera was *Ernani*, which the Metropolitan finally managed to wrest from San Francisco, presenting it as the jewel in the crown of that season. With *Ernani*, Pavarotti's catalogue of débuts came to an end. He was none the worse for wear, despite having sung Mozart and Verdi in close succession.

Milan, La Scala Opera Season 1985/86: Aida – *With Maria Chiara. (© Lelli & Masotti)*

Milan, La Scala Opera Season 1985/86: Aida – *With Maria Chiara and Ghena Dimitrovna. (© Lelli & Masotti)*

A BITTER EVENING

The list of great names that have been forced to endure the slings and arrows of the most dreadful upper gallery in the world – that of La Scala – is a long one. Del Monaco, Di Stefano, Bastianini, Callas, Carteri, Tebaldi, Freni, Scotto, and Katia Ricciarelli are only a few of them. To some extent Parma is also a contender for this record of cruelty, but its victims are generally much less illustrious. Whereas famous singers really have to perform in the most famous opera house in the world, they can easily avoid the risks of appearing at the Teatro Regio in Parma.

In 1983 Pavarotti's name would unexpectedly join the list of eminent unfortunates. This inauspicious event occurred during the performance of an opera in which he had always enjoyed undisputed success – *Lucia di Lammermoor*.

La Scala was going through a particularly difficult time. For some years Cesare Mazzonis and I had been assisting Maestro Siciliani with artistic direction. We worked in an atmosphere of uncertainty, trying to fill the gaps that kept appearing in the programme.

The worst case was Montserrat Caballé, who postponed her appearance in *Anna Bolena* and then quit after the first, turbulent performance. Not a day went by without the press drawing attention to the theatre's difficulties, and the dreaded upper gallery was very much on edge, ready to explode from one minute to the next at the slightest opportunity.

However, despite the knife-edge atmosphere in Piermarini's auditorium, the production of *Lucia di Lammermoor* was finding favour with the public, with its beautiful costumes by Missoni, Pizzi's excellent direction, and Maag's sure touch with the orchestra. Luciana Serra, making her Milan début, had gone down well for her assured performance and the purity of her vocal timbre.

Luciano had displayed a finely sculptured roundness of sound and phrasing in the first act, and been cheered in the wedding scene. The performance seemed set to restore the season's ailing fortunes; Siciliani was smiling, a rare sight, and was even leaning out of his stage-box.

Pavarotti began the final scene. The aria "Tombe degli avi miei", always one of his best, delighted the audience in every part of the theatre. The upper gallery in particular now seemed to be entirely and unreservedly on his side. Ardent cries and calls for an encore rained down from above for several minutes. Luciano acknowledged these with evident emotion, his mouth open in that curious way of his, almost as if he wanted to eat up all the applause and shows of affection.

At last the show was allowed to go on. By now there were only a few pages left, and with an inspired air about him he attacked the last, divine melody, "Tu che a Dio spiegasti l'ale". I was feeling completely relaxed by this stage, all my initial tension gone, and I was looking forward with professional interest to the F sharps in the words "O bell'alma innamorata", so that I could watch how he positioned the "mask" for those crucial *passaggio* notes between the registers.

Suddenly I felt a strange sensation, which brought to mind a distant nightmare – the final of the first Peri competition. His voice was losing colour and intensity, just as it had then, and for a few interminable beats it seemed, inexplicably, to become feeble. As an icy sweat broke out over my body, I glanced at Siciliani, seeking comfort. But the Maestro's face had gone white, and he had already slid to the back of the box, anticipating the disaster that was about to strike.

Luciano's *défaillance* did not last for more than a few seconds. As he explained to me later, it was to do with a breath that went wrong. His diaphragm, for some unfathomable reason, did not respond as promptly as usual, interrupting the flow of air needed to sustain the difficult phrase. But even before he had a chance to recover, all hell broke loose. The gods, who only a few minutes earlier had sung his praises, now condemned him mercilessly, whistling, hurling insults and lurid terms of abuse. I have never admired his sang-froid and his good sense more than I did at that moment. While famous colleagues in similar situations have lost their composure, reacting with aggressive gestures and even audible oaths, Luciano bowed repeatedly, spreading his arms wide in what was unambiguously a gesture of apology.

His response was unexpected, and very much appreciated, for the complaints ceased as suddenly as they had begun. When the curtain fell, I rushed to the stage to offer him some consolation. I tried to find something to say that might sweeten this bitter experience. I could think of nothing better than to condemn the behaviour of the upper gallery.

Laconically he replied, "My friend, the public is always right". And, as he always did during difficult times, he went off to get over his distress in solitude.

THE CONCERTS

Pavarotti's concert appearances can be subdivided into three categories:
1) Concerts with piano accompaniment
2) Vocal-Symphonic concerts
3) Concerts of opera arias, with orchestral accompaniment.

Concerts with piano accompaniment
I have already stressed the importance of the concerts leading up to his début in 1961 for testing and adjusting his technique.

His fierce competitiveness with John Allen, the other tenor in Campogalliani's school, urged him to give his very best from the start, so as not to compare unfavourably with his older, more experienced colleague.

Campogalliani's cast lists for his tours of the provinces were rather unusual. The main purpose was to reward his best pupils by giving them the chance to perform in public, so the classic concert form of soprano, tenor, baritone, bass (or mezzo-soprano) was not necessarily adhered to.

There were almost always two tenors (Pavarotti and Allen), two sopranos (Mirella Freni and Raffaella Ferrari) and sometimes a baritone (Enzo Consuma, occasionally replaced by Adelino Cordioli); very rarely there was a mezzo-soprano (Gabriella Panizza) and extremely rarely a bass (which might be Dmitri Nabokov).

These evening performances were electrifying, with vocal duels of a very high standard. Freni and Pavarotti were determined to prevail by their youth and freshness against John Allen and Raffaella Ferrari, whose vocal merits, on the other hand, were highly respectable, and who had no intention of ceding ground to their younger rivals.

In the concert mentioned earlier, which took place in the Teatro Parrocchiale di San Faustino in Modena, Freni and Pavarotti appeared together for the first time, in a long series of duets and arias, accompanied by me on the piano.

Before I go on to the official concerts, I want to relate a curious episode that occurred in Ostiglia, a little town on the banks of the Po. On this occasion there was only one spectator in the hall, and the disconsolate organisers decided to refund his ticket and cancel the concert. This is rather amusing in the light of Pavarotti's later performances, when there was always a frantic rush to buy tickets.

The two concerts in Moscow in 1964, with Alberto Ventura and Antonio Tonini at the piano, were significant because Herbert von Karajan was able once again to confirm Pavarotti's great talent; soon after this he offered him his début at La Scala in *Bohème*.

While the period between 1972 and 1985 certainly produced his most important concerts with piano, the importance of his early American recitals, with Masiello, Kohn and Wustman at the piano, is not yet fully appreciated in music circles. Because of Pavarotti's authority and prestige, these recitals ensured that a musical repertory hitherto enjoyed only by a refined minority of listeners was widely heard. Chamber music for voice and piano has never enjoyed great popularity, except in Germany and the Anglo-Saxon world. Although the great composers of each era have all contributed to an immense musical heritage, chamber recitals, even by great singers, used to attract very sparse audiences until only a few decades ago. Through his concerts, in which three quarters of every programme was chamber music, Pavarotti reached hundreds of millions of listeners, aided by his enormous popularity and his intelligent use of television. He deserves credit for the fact that many more people are now familiar with a genre which had always, unjustly, been exiled to the fringes of musical life.

Vocal-Symphonic concerts

Pavarotti's first work of this type was performed in 1961, the year of his début. It was Lorenzo Perosi's *Natale del Redentore*. Once a very popular composer, Perosi is almost forgotten today. Defined by some as a late post-Wagnerian, (what, then, do we call Richard Strauss?) the pompous and impassioned style of his writing for voices was a severe challenge for the young tenor's vocal capabilities.

In 1966 he had his first encounter with that great masterpiece, Verdi's *Requiem*. It was a special occasion – the official commemoration of Arturo Toscanini at La Scala – and Karajan's invitation helped to boost his rising fame. The music-lovers of Milan were looking forward with great excitement to hearing the young Pavarotti and judging him, particularly on his attack in "Hostias" – those celestial notes that were the hallmark of Carlo Bergonzi, at that time unrivalled in performances of the *Requiem*.

Pavarotti was worried; he had rehearsed those E naturals a thousand times, that magical major 3rd that seems to close the portals of infinity above the bows' impalpable tremolo. Despite endless practice he was still not satisfied. Minutes before the concert was to begin, he had not decided whether to sing that blessed note open or "covered".

As he explained afterwards, Karajan's hypnotic energy had him spellbound, eliminating every concern about technique, allowing the music to obey his spirit. And so it proved: the E natural issued forth with supernatural poetic grace, and the whole phrase unfolded with a legato of such longing that even the conductor was moved. After the performance he gave Luciano a photograph of himself with the dedication, "To the greatest tenor in the world".

The following year he attempted Rossini's vocal music for the first time, under the guidance of Carlo Maria Giulini at the RAI Auditorium in Rome. The brilliance of his timbre enhanced the beauty of the *Stabat Mater* in an extraordinary way, and the D flat, which is often prudently omitted, was reached with his usual ease.

The Seventies saw the public performance of the last vocal-symphonic work in his repertoire: Donizetti's *Requiem* at the Teatro Filarmonico in Verona. On that occasion I was impressed by the speed of his learning. He had just returned from America and was expected in Verona the following day, without yet knowing a single note of the "Ingemisco". As he was too tired to study it at the piano with me, he asked if I would make him a recording of myself singing and playing this demanding passage. I set about it reluctantly. My voice could be most generously described as bass-baritone at best; by using falsetto, however, I managed a more or less reasonable rendering of that difficult *tessitura*. Luciano was satisfied and amused by my efforts, and retired to his bedroom to listen to the improvised recording. He emerged two hours later, knowing the piece by heart and, he assured me, having had time for a good sleep as well.

Concerts of opera arias with orchestral accompaniment
There is little to recall of his youthful activity in this sphere, apart from his Paris début at the Salle Pleyel in 1965, where he was joined by Freni and the conductor Nello Santi. Despite the evening's success, Luciano was not spared a sarcastic and cruel jibe by Clarendon, the *Figaro*'s dreaded critic, who wrote in his ponderous style that as in a game of Chinese Shadows, Nello Santi's backside resembled Pavarotti's face and vice-versa. It was not long before the magic of his voice would silence such snide and tasteless remarks from newspaper hacks.

As his fame grew, so did his involvement in concerts of this type. Herbert Breslin and Tibor Rudas were quick to recognise that his name had the power to draw immense crowds. They shrewdly sought out larger venues – amphitheatres, stadiums and major sports centres, instead of the usual theatres and concert halls. Luciano was a willing partner in all this; he loved those massive crowds and was passionately adored in return. These evening performances took place in an incandescent atmosphere, with an edge of hysteria that could be unnerving – a worthy subject of research by psychologists and sociologists.

Meanwhile, millions of people were introduced to great music. He has been criticised for including the occasional popular song in his programme. Few people realise that this was just one (sometimes necessary) concession to the taste of his audiences, who, for the most part, were attending a concert of operatic and symphonic music (which is not always easy to understand) for the very first time.

From 1986 onwards, his concerts with orchestra formed the main part of Pavarotti's artistic output. Each year until 2005/2006 I conducted between twenty and thirty of these concerts. Taking into account that each concert, including travel and rehearsals, took up at least five days, the sums soon add up: 150 to 200 days a year devoted to concert activities, excluding the recitals with piano accompaniment.

There are hardly any countries where Pavarotti did not perform; and since television enormously extended the scope of these events, it is easy to understand the world-wide fame he achieved.

I remember a concert we gave at the Eiffel Tower. A few minutes before I went out to conduct the first piece in the programme, the Symphony from Verdi's *Luisa Miller*, Luciano asked me coolly: "Do you know how many people will be watching you tonight?". And in response to my questioning look he said: "Only 950 million". I felt myself go pale, and tried not to think about it.

When I returned to the wings after the Symphony, so that we could go on again together for his first piece, I noticed that he, too, looked a little pale. But five seconds before going on, his kindly face was transformed, taking on an expression of determination and maximum concentration I have seen in so many great artists in the moment before they face their audience.

His progressive abandonment of the stage in favour of this kind of performance can easily be explained by the huge numbers of spectators involved. For the first time in operatic history a singer could mesmerise billions of spectators, not only throughout Europe but in places as distant as São Paolo, Rio de Janeiro, Buenos Aires, Seoul, Hong Kong, Tokyo, Sidney, Auckland and Kuala Lumpur.

THE RECORDINGS

Pavarotti's commercial potential was swiftly recognised by the Decca company, who brought out what has been very aptly described as "a torrent of recordings". Barely two years after his début in *Bohème* in Reggio Emilia he was offered his first 45 rpm recording, consisting of five arias: the three from *Rigoletto*, plus "Lucean le stelle" and "Che gelida manina", directed by Edward Downes. While this little record did attract some curiosity and interest from music experts, it had a particular significance for Luciano. After listening to a studio recording of his own voice for the first time, Pavarotti instantly corrected a number of defects that he had not been aware of before then. He cut out numerous plaintive *portamenti*, which would later be thoroughly eradicated during his studies with Campogalliani, and speeded up his somewhat slack phrasing, making it more alive, contemporary and exciting.

A number of people who write about music are convinced – and have convinced their readers – that making records is some kind of sinecure, a far easier task than treading the boards of the stage. This is far from true. Recording companies work to a rigid timetable, often linked to the orchestras' requirements, and the work must be completed within the allotted time. Failure to complete a recording can lead to heavy financial loss, which the recording managers, naturally, do not look upon kindly. Those who fail to obtain a satisfactory result run the risk of being unceremoniously dropped. Hence, the recording session puts the artist's nervous system under considerable strain, allowing for no more than three takes for each track. One might suppose that three chances must always be better than the one, unrepeatable chance given in the theatre. But the microphone relentlessly captures even the slightest hint of catarrh, a hurriedly-taken breath or a tiny error in pronunciation – things that go completely unnoticed in the ample spaces of the theatre. This is why it is not easy to make records, contrary to what many people believe.

Some famous singers have been seized by panic when faced with the microphone. One of the first names that comes to mind is Franco Corelli, who suffered from attacks of nerves that made recording almost impossible, particularly during his first visit to a studio. Gianni Raimondi, another renowned tenor, has left far too few testimonies of his glittering vocal splendour, because the sight of a microphone would lead to instant psychological block. Piero Cappuccilli, who had one of the most extraordinary baritone voices of all time, compares unfavourably with other baritones who were better versed in the particular techniques of making recordings. I could continue at length about other singers.

Pavarotti, on the other hand, was a quick learner. In the lead-up to his next recording, *Beatrice di Tenda*, released in 1967, he mulled over the various defects in the recording he had made three years earlier. In the role of Orombello, with Sutherland co-starring, his singing is already much sharper. Orombello is not one of the great tenor roles – in fact Pavarotti never sang it on stage – but this second recording shows evidence of a much more diligent and thoughtful approach.

In *L'amico Fritz*, released in 1968, which we prepared for at length with Mirella Freni, he is almost perfect. The conductor was Gianandrea Gavazzeni, who imbued the opera with a deeply sympathetic understanding of Mascagni which makes this recording extremely interesting and novel, even today.

The true Pavarotti is revealed, with all the beauty and sumptuousness of his vocal capabilities, in his fourth recording, *La Fille du Régiment*, with Sutherland in 1968. Referring earlier to his stage début, I stressed what Pavarotti represented then in the operatic world: a full voice tenor, with a thrilling sound, who could effortlessly reach *tessiture* which until then had been braved only by light tenors.

This recording has bequeathed to us an example of prowess and of vocal "exploits" never before heard, and possibly never to be repeated for many years to come.

His first proper recital was also in 1968, and among these opera extracts Pavarotti clinches his supremacy in the high register, with "Spirto gentil" and the aria from *Don Sebastiano*, "Deserto in terra".

Another 1968 recording was Verdi's *Messa da Requiem*, conducted by Sir Georg Solti. This was the year when Pavarotti was truly launched on the record market. On this recording Pavarotti achieves an arcane, almost mystical depth of interpretation which is quite miraculous, particularly in the sections "Ingemisco" and "Hostias."

1970 produced three recordings: *Der Rosenkavalier*, with Solti conducting once again, which won an Italian music critics' prize; *Un ballo in maschera*, conducted by another eminent Italian, Bruno Bartoletti, with Renata Tebaldi in her one and only appearance as Pavarotti's partner; and Verdi's *Macbeth*, which he never performed on stage for the usual reason – the lack of prominence of the tenor role, despite the splendid aria "Ah, la paterna mano".

In 1971 he recorded just one long-playing record, an important one nevertheless: it included arias from *Guglielmo Tell*, *I Puritani*, *Il trovatore* and *La Gioconda*. We recorded most of these in London with the Philharmonia, and this was the first time I witnessed an entire orchestra express its delight at the exceptional artistic result Luciano achieved.

By 1972 Pavarotti was much in demand as a recording artist. The antiseptic conditions of the studio had no effect at all on the tonal beauty, the clarity of enunciation and the imaginative play of his interpretations. The recordings he made in 1972 immortalise on vinyl three of his most famous roles, in *Elisir d'amore*, *Lucia di Lammermoor* and *Rigoletto*; while Rossini's *Stabat Mater* is a fine demonstration of his facility in the upper register.

A singer's success is also measured by the number of compilations of famous arias they are asked to make. In 1973 his third solo LP was released, embossed with the medal of the Grand Prix Georges Thill. Among the curiosities on this record are two arias, "La fleur" from *Carmen*, and "Salut, demeure" from *Faust*, both sung in French, a language Pavarotti always struggled to master. Apart from his debatable pronunciation, the artistic result is perfectly respectable.

After this he recorded *Turandot* with Sutherland, Caballé and Mehta, then *La bohème* with Karajan and Freni. By now Pavarotti was becoming king of the gramophone record market, with two further solo albums, *The King of the High C's* and *Pavarotti in Concert*. One could criticise this last record (though very few have done) for its arbitrary orchestral arrangement of music originally written for voice and piano. But by this time Decca, to whom Pavarotti remained most faithful, had realised that it was in possession of some kind of King Midas, whose vocal cords could turn any piece of music into gold.

In 1975, after recording *Madama Butterfly* with Freni and Karajan, he made one of his most beautiful records of all, *I Puritani*. For a tenor, the role of Arturo, together with that of Arnoldo in *Guglielmo Tell*, represents what Paganini's *Capricci* might be to a violinist, or Liszt's transcendental *Études* to a pianist: compositions that are almost prohibitively difficult, accessible only to a few exceptional musicians, the kind one gazes upon in astonished admiration right from the early years of their studies.

Thus Pavarotti takes his place in the tiny circle of tenors who have managed to include in their repertory the opera that Bellini wrote for Rubini's mythical voice. What is more, he is probably the only 20th Century tenor who manages to reach the note everyone considers impossible – the

F natural in the *concertato* "Ella è tremante, ella è spirante." The composer inserted this note for the benefit of the last castrato singers – a final homage to that inhuman type of voice which was fortunately beginning to go out of fashion.

After his prodigious achievements in *Puritani* came a record of duets with Sutherland, Decca's other great star, which includes the rarely heard duet from *Linda di Chamounix*, as well as early examples of his approach to Verdi's grand operatic style in excerpts from *Aida* and *Otello*.

Towards the end of 1974, after a performance of *Bohème* at the Staatsoper in Hamburg, which had brought our threesome together again in the same cast, I spoke to Mirella and Luciano about an idea I had been nurturing for some time. Why not pool our efforts and experience to start a recording company that would operate outside the usual logic of market forces, and make more intelligent and refined choices. Mirella and Luciano liked the idea.

Nobly, Decca did not make too many objections to what they probably saw as a momentary whim on the part of one of their most prominent artists, and they allowed a few concessions in their highly restrictive contract of exclusive rights. And so we produced a variety of recordings on our label, CIME, beginning with a series of teaching records including the *Scuola di canto Freni-Pavarotti* (the Freni-Pavarotti Singing School) which we enriched with a record of Pavarotti-Ricciarelli duets, later adding a series entitled *Le grandi voci dell'Arena di Verona* (Great Voices of the Arena di Verona).

The refined, scholarly pieces we had selected for the *Scuola di canto* series continued with Rossini's *Petite Messe Solennelle*, recorded in 1977 (Freni, Pavarotti, Valentini Terrani, Raimondi, Magiera on piano, and Gandolfi conducting the Coro della Scala,) and with Donizetti's *Requiem* (Pavarotti, Cortez, Bruson, Washington). After further recordings of a repertory that was rather rarefied for the time, we were obliged to return to less élitist productions: *Pavarotti Recital*, with me at the piano, and *Mirella Freni-Luciano Pavarotti*, which I directed in 1980. Our falling sales figures, which had been causing concern, improved significantly with these last two recordings. However, our entrepreneurial venture encountered increasing difficulties, and we ended up accepting Decca's offer to buy the CIME catalogue. Once subjected to Decca's mighty distributive power, our recordings were suddenly successful. It seemed like magic, but of course it was simply that our lame and ailing sales network had not been up to the job.

1976 saw the release of *Maria Stuarda*, with Sutherland in the title role, which they never performed in the theatre, and of *Luisa Miller* with Caballé. Next came an enchanting LP that had enormous commercial success, *O holy night*. This became a gold disc, then platinum too.

1977 beat every record, with eight new releases, although most of these were compilations. Outstanding among these was *Il trovatore* with Sutherland, which was to feature in other compilations in later years.

In 1978 there were six releases, of which the only completely new recordings were *Cavalleria* and *Pagliacci* conducted by Gavazzeni, and *La favorita*, featuring Cossotto.

Six more records followed in 1979. At this point it has to be said that Decca showed inexhaustible imagination in presenting Luciano in every possible way: in duets, transcriptions, partnerships with other tenors (*Great tenors of today*), Neapolitan songs, verismo arias, even *La Gioconda Gala*, where his presence was almost marginal. While these moves were clearly commercially motivated, they were also a sign of his unprecedented success.

Bologna, July 1989 – With Riccardo Chailly. (© 1989, Judith Kovacs)

In 1980 he recorded Rossini's *Guglielmo Tell* with Freni and Riccardo Chailly; like *I Puritani*, this record would come to represent a milestone in the history of tenor role interpretations. Arnoldo's impassioned phrases and high notes, those "tongues of flame that seem to want to reach the heavens" (as Bruno Barilli described them in a performance by Giacomo Lauri Volpi) found in Pavarotti their ideal interpreter, uniquely capable of sustaining the thrilling romantic impetus of the piece.

In the same year Cetra published an item for connoisseurs, Verdi's *Pagine inedite*, conducted by Claudio Abbado in his characteristically informed and illuminating style.

Endless miscellanies followed, with alluring titles such as *Pavarotti's Greatest Hits*, *My Own Story*, and *Met Stars at Christmas*.

Seven more records appeared in 1981, including a genuine *Gioconda* with Caballé conducted by Bartoletti. There was also *Un ballo in maschera* with Ricciarelli and Patané, *La traviata* with Sutherland, and a further stream of *The Best of Pavarotti*, *Live from Lincoln Center* and so on, not forgetting the soundtrack from the film *Yes Giorgio*.

In 1982 Decca restricted themselves to just three Pavarotti releases,

Milan, La Scala Opera Season 1986/87: Un ballo in maschera. *(© Lelli & Masotti)*

possibly to avoid flooding the market. Of these, *La sonnambula* is worth noting, since it offers an opportunity to hear Pavarotti in an opera that he quickly removed from his theatre repertoire.

Six more records were issued in 1983; while 1984, alongside titles such as *Mamma*, *Napoli* and *Aria di Natale*, brought two significant recordings, *Mefistofele* and *Andrea Chénier*, which he had not yet performed on stage.

Seven records followed in 1985: *Passione*, *Ten Famous Tenors*, *The Bing Years*, another *Napoli*, *Un palco all'Opera*, *Alla mia città*, and, worth noting, a new *Ballo in maschera* conducted by Georg Solti.

1986 was the twenty-fifth anniversary of the start of his career. The first release that year was a *Traviata* from 1965, with Renata Scotto. After that came an uninterrupted series of compilations, almost all of them dedicated to the anniversary.

As this *résumé* has shown, Pavarotti's monumental output of audio-recordings is hard to equal: thirty operas, four major symphonic works, and an impressive number of recitals, duets and compilations – a total of 54 up to 1986.

TWENTY-FIFTH ANNIVERSARY

The twenty-fifth anniversary of the start of Pavarotti's career was celebrated in Modena with a performance of *La bohème* on 16th May 1985. It was an emotional evening – an important one for me too, since it marked my return to the podium after many years' absence.

If I am to explain the crucial role Pavarotti played in my decision to resume conducting, I have to go into a few of the personal events that took place in the years leading up to 1985.

In my efforts to assist my wife in her international career, I had begun, almost without realising it, to neglect my own artistic activities. There was another problem too. I had an obstinate and insurmountable reluctance to fly. This had prevented me from putting all kinds of plans into practice, including participating in Luciano's early, triumphal, American tours. My only two attempts at air travel had ended disastrously. When it was time to fasten seat-belts, I had been seized by a panic attack and had fled down the aircraft steps only seconds before their removal. I was almost mistaken for a terrorist, for in the heat of my escape I had forgotten my bags and passport.

After these episodes I thought it best to take on a lighter workload. I was particularly keen to avoid setting foot on an airplane again. And so I returned to the quiet life of a chorus master for several years, until Francesco Siciliani invited me to take up the post of Artistic Secretary at the Teatro alla Scala. Subsequently I became Director of Music Programming at the Maggio Fiorentino festival, and I would soon have taken on the management of some official body or other if events had not changed my life once more.

I had not given up playing the piano in any sense, but I had limited my playing to daily practice and concerts with distinguished singers, provided they were in Europe, and at venues easily reached by train or car.

Pavarotti continued to request my collaboration whenever he returned to the old continent, and we gave some memorable concerts together at La Scala, in Salzburg, Vienna, Paris, Madrid, and so on. Whenever we met, he never failed to rebuke me for having given up a fuller and more satisfying working life.

In the meantime Mirella Freni and I had divorced, and I had met Lidia, who became my second wife. Patiently and with great tenacity Lidia, who is a qualified doctor, devoted herself to helping me reveal the subconscious motives for my anxiety about travelling by air. In March 1985, when Luciano telephoned me from America, this rudimentary psychoanalytic therapy had already produced notable results. The telephone had rung insistently at 3:20 am. I heard Luciano's voice, somewhat altered. He must have fallen out with the orchestra conductor of *La bohème*, which he had just performed in Philadelphia, because he deluged me with a series of insults relating to my fear of flying. I wasn't offended by this form of salutation; we both come from Modena, where people have the strange custom of greeting each other with affectionate insults, in some cases even wishing each other the most atrocious diseases. But although I was still half-asleep, I sensed that there was something more than conventional greetings behind his curses.

Suddenly he made a proposal. "Listen," he said, "what would you say to our repeating, in Modena, the *Bohème* we did twenty-five years ago? It's about time you stopped this desk-work of yours and decided to be a serious musician. But remember, if you accept Modena you must also accept Genoa and Peking. It'll be the same production, and there's no chance of more rehearsals. Peking means getting on an airplane. So – either take it or leave it."

Judging from the final, unprintable and extremely fond insult he hurled at me, I could tell that he was expecting my usual obstinate refusal. I surprised him, and myself, as I said in a firm and decisive voice: "You can count on it. See you in a few days in Modena for the start of rehearsals".

It might seem that my decision was a risky one, but I had in-depth knowledge of this opera, having conducted it many times, and I had matured as a person and as an artist.

It was not easy, however, to pick up the baton again. Conducting requires intensive physical training, quick reflexes, and mastery of one's nervous system. This does not come out of the blue.

While there is hardly any distance between a pianist's finger and the key, so that sound can be produced a fraction of a second after the brain gives the command, an orchestra conductor's reaction time is longer, because the trajectory that the arm must make between the preparatory movement – upwards – and the performance movement – downwards – is longer.

However quick a conductor's and orchestra's reflexes might be, we are still talking about hundredths of a second – a lapse of time that would sometimes seem eternal to me, especially when dealing with some of Luciano's lightning attacks, seized as he was by the bohemian poet Rodolfo's romantic inspiration.

To give a practical example: in the finale of the first act, the attack of "Dammi il braccio, mia piccina…" is introduced by the violas' sustained G natural on the last beat of the bar (marked as no. 1 in the music below). The next beat has a quarter note rest (no. 2), after which the tenor enters on the second beat of the bar (no. 3); the second violins come in on the second eighth note of the third beat (no. 4), and the first violins on the last beat (5).

Usually the conductor pauses a moment on the held G natural; then tries to meet the tenor's eye to ensure that everything is in place with the action on stage; that done, he signals the first quarter note rest and proceeds with the tenor attack on the second beat of the bar.

Luciano would blatantly ignore this whole issue. Instead of facing me he would often launch into "Dammi il braccio" with his back to the audience, making it very difficult for me to catch the beginning of the second beat, especially as I hadn't yet signalled the first one! Moreover, one time he would sing "Dammi il braccio, mia piccina..." in a slow, sensual way; another time he would almost "gobble" the second quarter note as though in a sudden fit of erotic passion, so that I suddenly had to beat two quarter notes at supersonic speed. I dealt with the problem

Sanremo. A recital with Leone Magiera. (Photo Pablo Rossi)

by moving the fermata of the last quarter note to the first quarter note of the next bar, thus avoiding having to beat the initial quarter note, and everything fell smoothly into place.

There were other similar issues that I had to resolve in the course of rehearsals. These were problems arising not from the whims of a famous singer, but from a need for artistic truth, the need to delve into the character's psychology, and we went to great lengths to resolve them to our mutual satisfaction.

The days passed, and so did the rehearsals and performances, first in Modena, then in Genova, with Fiamma Izzo and Kallen Esperian alternately in the role of Mimì, and Sandra Pacetti as Musetta.

Finally, inexorably, came the day of departure for the great journey to Peking. The closer it came, the harder it was for me to sleep. My delirious nocturnal fantasies could easily have featured in a horror story by Edgar Allan Poe or a chapter from Erica Jong's *Fear of Flying*. I often imagined my body strewn in thousands of pieces over the grass around the runway; or else I saw myself thrashing around desperately amid flames and smoke, unable to move from my seat, trapped by a jammed seat belt. Then my thoughts would invariably go to the disaster at Orly, where Guido Cantelli lost his life.

At other times I would imagine the terrible fate of the passengers on board the DC9 at Ustica, and wonder how I would have behaved in such a crash. Then I would be terrified by the thought of a bomb on board, imagining, with my heart in my mouth, that hopeless 10,000 metre drop. Among these charming thoughts was even the idea that the pilots' food might be poisoned, leaving the passengers abandoned to their own devices in a runaway plane...

I had even made my will, having convinced myself that I had very little chance of surviving that very long flight (14 hours) from Genoa to Peking. I was also contemplating the possibility of returning from China by train, if I couldn't face the return journey by air. At any rate, I had put my personal affairs in order, which calmed me a little.

My daughter Micaela knew all my little secrets: the important documents hidden in the grand piano and the FIAT shares in the safe. As I handed her the keys I saw that my terror had transferred to her too; when I said goodbye to her for what I thought was the last time, her face was white and she was fighting back her tears.

Nevertheless, I was determined to keep my word, and on the morning of our departure I arrived at Genoa's Cristoforo Colombo airport in good time. The departure lounge was unbelievably full of orchestral musicians, members of the chorus and opera technicians, with a healthy number of Modenese supporters making up the rest of the expedition.

Like all people who are terrified by air travel, I was fully informed of the technical details of the Alitalia Jumbo we would all be boarding, and I wondered anxiously if it would be able to bear the weight of all those people, as well as their instruments, scenery, scores, personal baggage and who knows what else.

Luciano never left me on my own, not even for a second, having given me encouragement throughout the car journey from Modena to Genoa. A few minutes before the call to board, seeing that my teeth were beginning to chatter spasmodically, Lidia made me swallow a white pill that had a rapid and almost miraculous effect; so much so that I stepped decisively onto the plane, to the surprise of Luciano and the theatre directors Alberti, Terracini and Levrero, who were clearly worried that I was about to make a run for it.

We took our seats in the Top Class of the Jumbo: a most luxurious place, twelve seats in all, where gracious stewardesses seemed intent on satisfying our every desire.

Lidia's magic pill continued to have its effect, and I felt almost relaxed. When a few minutes later the captain's voice announced that we had to evacuate the plane immediately because of a bomb alert, I maintained a certain dignity.

I have to say that my guardian angels, Lidia and Luciano, behaved commendably, grasping me under the arms and heading for the exit

Pesaro, July 1989. (© 1989, Judith Kovacs)

briskly but without panic. They certainly could not have guessed that according to my contorted logic this unexpected hitch was actually a relief, a guarantee of thorough checks and therefore less danger ahead.

There was widespread panic, however, among the rest of the passengers. The small contingent from Liguria-Emilia was fleeing wildly through every available exit, swearing and praying to the good Lord.

We went back to the departure lounge and sat down again. I was amazed by my behaviour – I even comforted a Bulgarian violinist who had been seized by uncontrollable bouts of vomiting and was determined to run away. Finding someone more frightened than myself gave me a sense of relief.

We waited three hours for a thorough search to be carried out, at the end of which no bomb was found.

Finally we re-embarked; a second pill renewed my courage, and the huge Jumbo, powerful and majestic, took off for China, dispersing its white slipstream to the winds over the Ligurian Sea, and with it my extravagant and – luckily – unfounded fears.

PART TWO

THE TOUR OF CHINA

That dreadful night between 5th and 6th September 2007 I suffered from a continuous series of distressing nightmares. All my oldest fears seemed to have resurfaced in my subconscious: one minute there was a troop of German SS soldiers with machine-guns surrounding our country villa to arrest my father; then a gigantic wave was engulfing the old Queen Elizabeth taking me on my first voyage to America; to cap it all, I was being served breakfast aboard a 747 Jumbo Jet that was on fire and falling headlong into the Atlantic Ocean. I wanted to shout, but couldn't, and my heart was beating like mad; so it was a relief when the phone rang and rescued me from these terrifying nightmares.

Before answering, I glanced at the alarm clock beside my bed; it was ten past five, and I realised that reality was about to be far worse than all my most frightening dreams. It was Luciano Ghelfi, speaking quickly and to the point: "Luciano died a few minutes ago. He never regained consciousness after your last visit". A few more quick words, and we ended the conversation. I dressed quickly, got into the car and drove from Bologna to Modena in record time, although the journey seemed to last forever, and my whole life flashed before my eyes in the space of an hour.

The radio and television crews were already there, and I was assailed by a swarm of reporters. I got past them with some difficulty, and was among the first people to pay homage to my friend, who was lying serenely on a large bed in his splendid villa on the outskirts of Modena.

My poor friend! He had only had a few months to enjoy the villa that he had so lovingly built, close to his restaurant and his beloved old riding-school where dozens of thoroughbreds had once taken part in international show-jumping competitions. For a moment I could almost see the agile and elegant riders of every nationality, competing in the San Marino Grand Prix; I could almost hear the panting of the horses as they approached the jumps; and see Luciano again, in the VIP enclosure, intently watching the prize-giving ceremony, perpetually besieged by photographers and beautiful girls.

Mournfully, I made my way home, my head filled with memories, thinking back to that day in 1985… the Jumbo Jet landing on the runway at Peking, carrying all the orchestra, chorus and technicians of the Teatro

Carlo Felice in Genoa, plus the soloists of the cast of *Bohème*, which we would be performing at the National Theatre in Peking. I was pleased at having finally defeated my fear of flying. Before leaving the aircraft I embraced Luciano and Adua who, together with my wife Lidia, had done a marvellous job in helping me overcome my psychological blocks. I had solemnly promised all my fellow travellers that if the flight went well I would kiss the soil of China as soon as I set foot on it, and thank the heavens for preserving us from harm.

I left the aircraft just in front of Luciano, who was wrapping his enormous colourful shawl around his neck, preparing to make his theatrical appearance on the steps. I did not really like the idea of kissing the runway, which was dirty and stank of burnt oil and kerosene; but a promise is a promise, and I kept my word, not just once but several times, to satisfy the crowd of photographers who had gathered on the runway.

Finally they loaded us into some old buses reminiscent of the vehicles circulating in Italy just after the Second World War. I caught sight of Luciano slowly descending the aircraft stairway, his arms making wide gestures of greeting, lit by the continual flash of cameras. A long, very luxurious black limousine awaited him; I found out later that it was reserved exclusively for visiting heads of state. We felt rather abandoned without his reassuring presence, but I shrugged off these feelings and glued myself to the window to discover a completely new world, the Far East, which I had dreamed of as a boy while reading books by Emilio Salgari, and which I was now seeing in real life.

However, reality is rarely quite as we imagine it to be. I could see flat countryside gliding by, with plantations bearing no resemblance at all to the Paduan plains of my homeland, and rice-fields quite unlike the ones around Vercelli and in Lomellina. What caught my attention most was the endless river of bicycles flowing like liquid at the side of the roads; each cyclist carrying a water-melon or two, carefully tied to the rear carrier.

Every so often the Chinese driver would overtake a mule-cart laden with foodstuffs, hooting his horn in perfect Neapolitan style. Sometimes we came across bigger carts, pulled by a horse with two mules following meekly behind it.

Without air-conditioning we all sweated profusely, and it was a very bumpy ride, much more so than our journey in the Alitalia Jumbo. Lidia tried to keep up our morale. "Cheer up! If I'm not mistaken we should be at the Fragrant Hills Hotel in a few minutes, and we can relax with a jasmine tea." Just then our pleasant guide and interpreter announced grandly, "Ladies and gentlemen, here is the Fragrant Hills Hotel".

Overcome with exhaustion, we all slept for a couple of hours. Then, a few at a time, we met up in the bar-restaurant, in the hope of getting some refreshment. But bitter disappointments awaited us. As Lidia had promised, there was plenty of jasmine tea. But our hearty appetites, accustomed mostly to Genoese, Modenese and Roman cooking, were not particularly satisfied by the Chinese cuisine, although the food was fine.

Lidia and I sought refuge in Luciano's room, hoping to find something more to our taste. I was stunned: it wasn't a room! It was an immense suite big enough for about fifty people. There was a vast dining room, luxuriously arrayed, and it seemed that a sumptuous meal awaited us.

I was delighted when I recognised a famous Genoese restaurateur, Zeffirino, flanked by two sturdy Italian cooks, giving brusque commands to a troupe of Chinese cooks.

Luciano, draped in an ample bathrobe, was supervising everything and tasting the dishes. He invited us to take our seats, magnanimous as a sultan. "Now, let's see if the menu is to your liking: pasta with pesto alla genovese, tournedos alla Rossini, grilled sea bass…"

"That's enough!" I exclaimed. "Do you know what they're serving in the Chinese restaurant? How are we going to survive for two weeks?"

"That's no problem; you can eat here all the time. In fact, do me a favour, you and Lidia, phone all the principal singers at once and invite them here."

No sooner said than done. The first person I contacted was Fiamma Izzo, who was lying in bed in utter despair.

"There's nothing I can eat here!"

"Don't worry. Tonight you're eating at Zeffirino's."

"Sure, in Piazza De Ferrari in Genoa! Are you trying to be funny?"

"Come to room 505 right now, and you'll see if I'm joking."

Fiamma arrived after a few minutes and broke into loud shrieks of joy. All the others – Servile, Scaltriti, Nuccia Focile – reacted in exactly the same way.

Zeffirino's cooking was simply amazing; the tournedos Rossini melted in the mouth, the *mille-feuille* was superb.

"But how did Zeffirino manage to bring all these wonderful things to China?" asked M.R., who was tucking in at a nearby table in pleasant company.

"Easy," said Luciano, "he stowed five enormous fridges filled with provisions in the hold of the jumbo."

"And what about the Chinese customs officials?"

"Either they turned a blind eye or they mistook the fridges for double basses! Zeffirino cunningly put the fridges in air-tight containers, none of which were opened."

"That was lucky. If they'd known what was in them we probably wouldn't be here enjoying these gastronomic masterpieces!"

Luciano laughed. "Yes, the American customs often confiscated tortellini, pigs' trotters and hams from me, claiming it's illegal to import meat into the U.S. They probably ate it all themselves."

I remember M. laughing wholeheartedly at this. She was a beautiful girl of about twenty-five, tall, blonde, with a well-proportioned face and gorgeous eyes, and she spoke seven languages fluently. As for her singing, it got better as the years went by. She was extremely good company and it was no surprise that many men fell for her. That evening I sensed a certain tension in the atmosphere. Every so often Adua would cast malevolent glances at M. and Luciano kept watching the budding friendship between M. and one of the other dinner guests with concern.

This did not prevent me from enjoying my dinner. Tomorrow was going to be a long hard-working day. I suspect that few people realise how much physical effort goes into conducting an orchestra. Not only is it tiring to stand for hours, but the torso is subjected to countless pressures, and the arms have to rotate continuously. Total concentration is needed; the mind focusing on the intricacies of the score, while the face communicates with the musicians. A conductor can lose a couple of kilos in a day of orchestra rehearsals. So, having eaten my fill at dinner that night, I stoked up the next morning before setting off for the rehearsal with a quarter of *torta pasqualina* – a Genoese Easter pie that deserves to be much better known.

The black limousine reserved for Luciano for the duration of his stay in China was waiting outside the Fragrant Hills Hotel. Lidia and I squeezed through the crowd that was waiting for Pavarotti and got into the car. It is impossible to imagine how popular Pavarotti was unless one has witnessed such scenes. He managed to get out of the hotel only with the help of numerous policemen and bodyguards, and the large car rocked as he fell heavily onto the back seat.

"Let's hope the same thing doesn't happen at the theatre," he muttered through clenched teeth. But inevitably a huge crowd was also waiting for him outside the stage door.

"We'll end up being an hour late for the rehearsal," I complained. We had just performed *Bohème* in Modena and Genoa, but that day of rehearsals was essential for us all. All it takes is a few days off, and an opera, like a complex machine, needs oiling and overhauling once again.

The Chinese fans were out of control. Luciano was swearing angrily as he struggled to extricate himself from their clutches and reach the entrance. Maybe his bulky frame reminded them of Buddha; they all wanted to touch him, as if to possess him physically, and for a few moments we feared for his safety.

"Right, we've done it at last," he panted, covered in sweat. "Let's take a look at this theatre."

It seemed more like a cinema than a theatre. We hurried along the corridors, Luciano trying to get to the stage, while I tried to find the podium, where I apologised to the orchestra for our unavoidable delay.

We started rehearsing. The orchestra of the Carlo Felice responded perfectly to my baton, and the singers all seemed in excellent form. In spite of their fresh voices and their high levels of ability (some went on to have brilliant careers), when Luciano "opened his valves" it was like hearing the roar of a Ferrari in comparison with the whine of an old Cinquecento. He was at the peak of his vocal maturity, and his young colleagues gazed at him almost open-mouthed, with enormous respect and admiration.

"Wake up, don't stand there like statues," Luciano bawled. "Come on, *Bohème* is an opera about young people, and you remind me of a whole lot of mummies!"

Spurred on by his vivid incitements, they finally got the feel of the acting Luciano wanted from them. He would urge them on by example, moving with unbelievable agility for a man of his size. He sang the whole rehearsal with full voice, reproving those who were saving their voice for the première, which was only three days away, after the dress rehearsal. "The voice needs to be kept fit, come on, let's go!" he roared at Fiamma Izzo, who tended to economise on her voice. He was an inspiration and a spur to everyone, to the orchestra as well, which put in a huge effort and produced wonderfully atmospheric sounds from Puccini's splendid score.

Finally the hour of truth was approaching – "*las cinco de la tarde*" for bullfighters, 9 pm for us musicians. Luciano and I made the rounds of the dressing rooms, to encourage the younger performers and wish them luck. They were all a little nervous, but generally very determined. Fifteen minutes before the start, dressed in my tails and bow tie, I went to find Luciano as usual for his vocalisation exercises. We began in the key of D major, with various arpeggios leading to the high A natural. Then he asked me, as always, to accompany him in "Recondita armonia", his favourite "exercise". His sustained F naturals in the opening phrases of the aria were full, rounded and "well-turned" (a term I have tried to explain in the technical appendixes).

"That's enough, don't you think? It seems all right."

"Yes, I'd say so. Well, good luck, and… see you in a few minutes." I hurried into the orchestra pit, ready to take my place on the podium. In those moments just before facing an audience, an artist tries to achieve maximum concentration; some pray, others do yoga exercises, I just detach myself from the drama of the occasion so that I can be as relaxed and calm as possible when I walk onto the podium. The Chinese callboy signalled to me to go on, and I set off on the short walk through the orchestra, with many of the musicians wishing me the customary "*in bocca al lupo*" ("break a leg") under their breath.

I was expecting the polite applause that always greets the conductor's appearance, but I was disappointed. Although the auditorium lights had been dimmed, the audience carried on talking loudly. Naturally, I could not understand a word, and after gesturing to the audience a few times for silence, I decided to begin the performance. As the curtain opened there was a prolonged "oooooh" of wonderment, and Marcello's opening lines, sung by the baritone Servile, almost silenced the auditorium. When Luciano opened his mouth, there was absolute silence for a few moments, then I heard a strange noise behind me. What looked like a human tsunami was approaching the fragile barrier between the orchestra and the public. I carried on conducting, but could not resist glancing over my shoulder, and what I saw was frightening. At the back of the auditorium, the spectators seated furthest from the stage were clambering over the heads and shoulders of the people in front of them, who, in turn, were trying to regain lost ground by repeating the same foolhardy manoeuvre. I seriously feared that they would end up toppling into the pit like a wall of dominoes, with unimaginable consequences for both conductor and orchestra.

Luciano quickly spotted the danger we were in. Having spent our childhood years during the last World War, we both had pretty sharp reflexes. His next move proved to be a very intelligent one. He came to

Leone Magiera, George Bush Sr. and Pavarotti. Seattle, 1989.

his first high B flat, on the words "l'idea avvampi in fiamma", and pitched it with the utmost beauty and power, holding it for much longer than Puccini had intended. Knowing at once what he was up to, I waited for him, my arms raised to hold back the orchestra, who probably weren't yet aware of the danger. They were watching me with surprise at this unexpected pause, which had the miraculous effect of placating the crowd. They discharged their pent-up excitement in lengthy applause.

Gradually, as if that B flat had acted as a tranquiliser, they all went back to their seats and we were able to continue the opera without further mishap.

Each high note was applauded, and there was total delirium after the C in "Che gelida manina". They were all out of their seats, jumping with joy, and we couldn't finish the aria – we had to leave out the last few bars. Meanwhile, poor Fiamma Izzo failed to get a single clap for the aria "Mi chiamano Mimì", despite its solemn ending and her beautiful rendering of the piece.

Over dinner "at Zeffirino's" we discussed what had happened. The singers, who could see the audience, had been fully aware of the risks posed by the surging masses. Luciano was declared the hero and saviour of the evening for his improvised trick of holding that top note *ad libitum.*

"I'm not God yet," he joked.

"But you are the god of tenors," more than one person replied.

Anyway, we paid him endless compliments, as did the Prime Minister and a delegation of Chinese, who had been invited to taste Italian cooking and to set up trading links with Italy.

We went to bed feeling rather euphoric. As I opened my door I caught a glimpse of someone stealing into M.'s room.

"I smell a rat," Lidia commented.

"Seven years have passed," I said.

"What do you mean?"

"G.'s relationship with Luciano also lasted seven years."

"And who was G.?"

"Did you never meet her? It's incredible that their love story never got into the gossip weeklies."

"They must have been very careful not to be found out."

"They were. Once at the Hotel Baglioni in Bologna, Luciano asked me to show my identity card instead of his. Then after a while, when the hall-porter wasn't looking, he went up to the room with G. If the Baglioni have kept a record of their guests, you'd see that officially I spent a night there with that gorgeous girl…" I refrained from saying her name, but Lidia didn't mind.

"And what would your first wife Freni have said if she had rummaged through the records of the Hotel Baglioni?"

"Nothing, because Mirella was there. She was slightly shocked, but in the end she found it amusing. We were all young and exuberant…"

"Well I'm certainly not going to be shocked! But what was G. like? Was she really that important to him?"

"If I told you that in terms of beauty and personality she beat M. by some way, you wouldn't believe me. And she had a good influence on the artistic choices he made. She encouraged him to sing *Puritani* and *Figlia del Reggimento*…"

"And did you get on well with her?"

"Very well indeed. I never got on so well with any of his other 'secretaries'. With G. you could talk about music seriously and in depth; with all the others you just talked generally, about nothing."

"Were there many others?"

"We mustn't gossip. I'm tired, I've got the weight of *Bohème* on my shoulders."

We had two free days, and we finally managed to see the main sights of Peking: the Forbidden City (featured in Bernardo Bertolucci's film, *The Last Emperor*), the Temple of the Sky, the Winter Garden and the Great Wall. They were truly unforgettable days. We had Luciano's limousine at our disposal, although he chose not to leave his room for fear of every singer's chief enemy – the common cold. In fact he had some very demanding rehearsing to do, for a recital with orchestra in the Great Hall of the People, hitherto reserved only for Government meetings. This would be a historic event for the Chinese.

A song recital with orchestra is a very particular genre, which is usually the preserve of eminent artists. It is more taxing than an operatic performance, since the singer bears the responsibility for the whole event. Some great singers of the past, such as Beniamino Gigli, used to share the programme with a soprano, and as he grew older, so did Pavarotti. But until then he gave solo recitals, consisting of at least ten songs.

The Great Hall of the People was enormous, and although the audience numbered at least fifteen thousand, Luciano did not resort to the use of microphones. It was a huge success. The conductor was Emerson Buckley, who had reached a ripe old age, but conducted very well, and the Carlo Felice orchestra played brilliantly.

Luciano stayed on for hours, signing autographs for the long queues of Chinese, which tailed back as far as Tienanmen Square.

"Who knows if he'll invite you to conduct one of these magnificent concerts one day," Lidia said. "Buckley seems very old and worn-out to me."

"*Mors tua, vita mea*. It's a fact of life, but I hope Buckley carries on for a long while. I'm happy conducting operas." I didn't know then that a few months later I would begin an endless round of concerts with Luciano that would see us spending over a thousand evenings together and flying non-stop all over the world.

A few days later we finished our performances of *Bohème* and we all left for Italy, except for Pavarotti, who stayed in China to film a documentary. He came to the airport to see us off, and I saw him upset as he watched M. leaving arm in arm with her new man. As Herbert Breslin also wrote in his book, Luciano then suffered a long period of depression, during which he even contemplated suicide.

ARGENTINA

Luciano's spirits only really began to revive when we were doing *Bohème* in Argentina. By this time we were working together in perfect harmony for at least nine months each year, with me either at the piano or conducting.

I realised that I was inexorably losing touch with many other famous singers with whom I had worked in the past: the delightful Katia Ricciarelli, whose *piano* was so artistic and exciting; the aggressive, sulky Renata Scotto, who knew exactly how to transform herself into a warm and passionate actress; the formidable Piero Cappuccilli, with his enormously deep breaths and his irresistible high notes; the touchy but supremely sensitive Renato Bruson; the aristocratic and slightly aloof Nicolai Gedda; my ex-pupil and friend, the irresistible Ruggero Raimondi... I was now completely engrossed in working with Luciano. I made a point of closely observing his ever-changing artistic and vocal development, as I was in constant touch with the man whom many considered to be "the greatest tenor of all time". I wanted to understand everything about his nature, even the most secret aspects of it.

His daily workload – excluding opera performance and concert days – consisted of more than just his regular practice with piano accompaniment. He was always thinking about his operatic roles, and consequently his vocal technique, in order to convey his favourite characters' states of mind as truthfully as possible.

It was not uncommon for him to stop in the middle of doing a crossword (one of his favourite pastimes), stare into space for several minutes, and then suddenly ask me a question such as, "Why do you think Puccini wrote 'Chi son' twice in 'Gelida manina'? Wasn't once enough?"

I would be caught unaware, possibly while reading a leading article in the *Corriere della Sera*, and I would ask him for a moment or two to think about it.

"That's a good question," I would say at last. "Perhaps he made the tenor voice come down strongly on the down beat so as to give extra thrust to the repetition of the second 'chi son' which resolutely introduces the distant modulation to F major."

Luciano would be mildly irritated by references to degrees of modulation and tonality. With his limited knowledge of musical notation and even lesser knowledge of the rules of harmony, the jargon meant little to him, and he would always end up accusing me of excessive intellectualism.

"No, I think it's much simpler: the first 'Chi son?' has to express a sense of bewilderment. Rodolfo, like all human beings, doesn't know exactly who he is or what he is doing here in this world."

"That's a question which all religions and all philosophies seek to answer."

"Yes of course. But I have to find in those two notes the vein of universal angst… Do you know what I mean? Give me the note, please."

I would play him the A flat, which transforms into a G sharp (woe betide me if I mentioned the word "enharmonic" – he would get furious). If there was no piano I would sing the note, since I am blessed with perfect pitch. He would practise over and over for a while, until I agreed that his aim had been fully achieved.

"And the second 'Chi son?'," I asked him.

"Oh, the second one is easier. Rodolfo has already understood in a flash that this kind of thinking has little effect on the mind of a simple girl like Mimì. So the second 'Chi son' must sound proud and self-confident. You see he says, 'I am a poet'. He needs to say this as if he were saying 'I am a Rockefeller, or an Agnelli, or a Bill Gates'! It's a clever way of impressing a simple-minded dressmaker's apprentice, don't you think?"

"Excellent. I see that your knowledge of feminine nature helps you to a better understanding of the characters."

He did not smile at my intended joke.

"It's life, my dear friend, life! That's what an operatic singer must bring out in every note. Otherwise, he's just wailing and doing vocal exercises, in time with metronomic signals from those awful beat-thumpers on the podium."

Luciano hated conductors on principle; he felt they wanted to deny his freedom of expression. Only a few were spared. He admired Herbert von Karajan, who openly expressed his own admiration for Luciano, Claudio Abbado, and Carlos Kleiber, who unfortunately admired him far less – Pavarotti was too "free" for his rather pragmatic tastes as a conductor. Immodestly, I felt that perhaps I too was among the chosen few, since I was almost always the conductor of his choice. I would never even compare myself with those giants, although (to hell with modesty) none of them was as good a pianist as I, with the exception of Claudio Abbado, who hardly ever played.

These exchanges took place at the Plaza Hotel in Buenos Aires (known as Baires to the locals). It was nearly time for me to go to the Teatro Colón for the first orchestra rehearsal. I asked Luciano, " Is it pronounced Còlon or Colón?"

"That's a good question, too. Try asking the taxi driver who's waiting for you downstairs. And let me know the names of the most famous Argentinian composers, as well. I want to mention them tomorrow at the press conference; I don't want to make a fool of myself. Right now I can only think of Astor Piazzolla…"

"I'll make you a list of the most famous ones, but now I have to go, time's getting on…"

"Ok then, see you this evening. Have a good rehearsal."

The taxi driver was of Italian origin, like many Argentinians, so I was able to put my query to him.

"*Señor*, I'm going to the Teatro Còlon," I said, deliberately putting the stress on the first "o". Smiling, he replied in perfect Italian, "You see, most of 'our' people use the wrong stress, as you have just done. Còlon refers to a part of the intestine, don't ask me exactly which part. The correct pronunciation is Colón, which is Cristoforo Colombo's surname, and means 'colonizer' or founder of a colony. In Spanish his full name is Cristóbal Colón, and the Spanish insist on believing that he is one of them."

"I see. I'll buy that book that was recently published about Columbus, written by Salvador de Madariaga, so I don't embarrass myself again."

Chatting pleasantly, we arrived at the theatre. I felt almost giddy as I looked at that exquisitely beautiful building, where so many of our great artists had given memorable performances. Among conductors, I thought of historic figures such as Ettore Panizza and Arturo Toscanini, and wondered how an orchestra accustomed to working with such gigantic figures would respond to me. At the first rehearsal an orchestra always tries to test the conductor by playing the odd wrong note to see if he will notice…

Judging from the rather warm reception I got from the members of the orchestra, I realised that they were mostly Italians. I made no attempt to show off my Spanish, which I had diligently brushed up. If they did try to catch me out with an out-of-place note it escaped my notice, but I suspect they didn't, because I have a pretty good ear. Anyway, they were extremely welcoming, and as the days went by I formed increasingly friendly relationships with many of them, particularly with the first violin.

"Do you know, Maestro, who added the bowing instructions to the score? It was Ettore Panizza himself, who knew Puccini well."

"And did Toscanini approve?"

"He didn't change a single marking."

"Then neither will I, since I am neither Toscanini nor Panizza," I said, laughing.

"Excuse me, Maestro," he said softly, coming up to me and changing the subject, "are you aware of the phenomenon of the *desaparecidos* (the disappeared) in this country?"

"I've heard of it. But you know, I'm always travelling around the world with Pavarotti, and I rarely get a chance to read Italian newspapers. Is it really that serious?"

"Very. And very frightening. I came here from Italy when I was eighteen; now I'm forty-six, but I'd gladly go back to our country. To tell the truth, I'm afraid for myself and for my family. If you happen to hear of a vacancy for a violinist in any theatre anywhere in Italy, I'd be most grateful if you would let me know."

"I'll certainly do that; have no doubt about it." We exchanged visiting cards. His name was Aldo Munaroni.

In the evening, when I got back to the hotel, I found Luciano in a bad mood, blowing his nose peevishly.

"I think I can detect the symptoms of a cold," he announced, rather melodramatically. I shuddered. If Pavarotti caught a cold this could cause havoc all over Buenos Aires, and much more besides. If a regular singer catches cold and has to miss the odd performance, no one makes a fuss. However, if the singer in question is called Pavarotti, and he misses his opening night because he has effectively lost his voice, all hell breaks loose in the media, with dreadful accusations aimed at all kinds of people. A prime example of such media uproar occurred when Maria Callas had to withdraw from *Norma* at the Rome Opera because she suddenly lost her voice after the first act; she was subjected to insults from the public, and the most violent attacks from the press, who also laid into the theatre, the management, and anything else they could think of attacking.

"Fortunately, my family arrives tomorrow. And my new secretary, J." Luciano's expression was ecstatic, like a lover's.

"Who?"

"J. I met her a month ago at the Vienna Opera. She was working in the theatre archive and I persuaded her to come here. She's a qualified phytotherapist."

"Meaning?"

"Herbal remedies, ignoramus! You musicians don't know about anything except notes!"

Modenesi often insult each other in jest, so I was not offended by his comment.

"And apart from phytotherapy? Tell me…"

"She gives very good massages, using various poultices…"

"What sort?" I asked, cheekily.

"Stop teasing. You'll see, she'll be able to cure my cold."

At lunch time the next day I was received by the Pavarotti family in its full glory: Adua, the perfect hostess, greeted me graciously, and the girls, Titti, Cristina and Giuliana, chattered happily around me.

At the table with us was a pretty girl, about twenty-two years old, who bowed to me in perfect Viennese style. I sincerely hoped she was not expecting to sing, because too often with M. I had been forced to argue until I was blue in the face to get out of having to accompany her singing displays.

After lunch I returned to the theatre for rehearsals. There was no sign of Luciano for a few days. He stayed in his room, rubbing pungent and acrid-smelling ointments on his chest, sniffing strange spices and inhaling herbal substances now and again.

His absence from rehearsals had not gone unnoticed, however, and the newspapers were spreading alarmist reports – as if there were nothing more serious happening at that time in Argentina! But Luciano turned up at the rehearsal before the dress rehearsal, and although he chose not to sing that day, the theatre directors felt reassured. They would probably have lost their jobs if he failed to perform, but to be on the safe side they had arranged for Luis Lima, a well-known and very able Argentinian tenor, to replace him if necessary.

By the dress rehearsal the situation had not changed much. Luciano did a lot of humming and coughing, and was replaced by Lima in the third act. The management of the Colón decided to allow three days between the dress rehearsal and the opening night, to give Pavarotti time to recover.

Even when I got into the car with Luciano to go the theatre on the evening of the première, I was unsure if he would sing, and I suspect he was too. I asked him frankly, and he said he would decide only after his usual warm-up in the dressing room. But then he left out the preliminary vocalizations, and asked me directly for his entry to "Recondita armonia".

At first he produced a gurgling that sounded like a night-time chorus of frogs. This scared him, and he said, "No, it's impossible. Let's go back to the hotel".

"First have another five or six tries."

"It's all very well for you to say that, but I'm choking."

He was reluctant to give up too easily, however. After a while he tried again. It went a bit better, but he said, "There are still a lot of frogs in my throat."

"They'll go away."

The conversation seemed surreal.

Just then there was a knock on the door, and Luciano flared up. "Who the hell's that bothering us now?" he roared.

"*El Señor Presidente de la República, Señor Pavarotti.*"

I opened the door. Fortunately President Alfonsín was following some way behind the advance guard and had not heard what Luciano said. He came in and immediately started thanking Luciano for deciding to perform in spite of being unwell.

"But we've still got Luis Lima ready to replace me, haven't we?"

"But that won't be necessary, *Señor* Luciano. You'll see, everything will be fine."

"Let's hope so, *Signor Presidente.*"

"Well, as they say in Italian, *in bocca al lupo*, good luck *Señor* Luciano."

"Thank you, *Signor Presidente.*"

Finally Alfonsín left the room.

"How can I not sing now?" asked Luciano in desperation.

"Come on. Let's carry on."

On the third attempt "Recondita armonia" came out almost pure, and Luciano gave a slight smile.

"Looks like the frogs are back in the pond. But what a huge risk, tonight!"

"Can I go down and change now?"

"Yes, but please come back fifteen minutes before we go on!"

I put on my tails, struggled as always with my white bow-tie, and retraced my steps. J. was with Luciano, rubbing his chest with the usual foul-smelling ointment.

"More vocalizations, Luciano?"

"No, what's done is done now. See you on stage."

Here I will end my tale of *Bohème* in Buenos Aires, because I run the risk of becoming monotonous if I keep recounting Luciano's triumphs. All I will add is that on this particular evening his triumph was even more outstanding than usual because of his sudden and unexpected recovery from a heavy cold.

Did Luciano have a particular aptitude for singing when he was unwell? He certainly did. His vocal apparatus was like a big diesel engine that kept running reliably through numberless operatic performances and concerts, right up to the fatal age of seventy.

He was unusual in being able to anticipate and forestall the flow of catarrh: if the obstruction was high up, he would position the voice more in the throat, but not too low; if it was heading for the throat, he would instantly bring the sound up, into the mask. He managed this of course not just by great technical mastery but also through the special configuration of his anatomy, for he happened to have unusually large resonating chambers.

Statistics show that there were very few occasions when he had to cancel a performance. When he did, the media were merciless, presenting him falsely as an unprofessional divo who failed to carry out his duties – the very opposite of the truth!

We left Buenos Aires to continue our almost unbroken round of concerts. Tibor Rudas, the Hungarian impresario, wanted to take full advantage of the Luciano gold-mine – his every appearance mustered between thirty thousand and five hundred thousand people, in stadiums, arenas or parks. The ticket prices were no joke either: over a thousand dollars for the best seats, of which there were plenty.

Every so often, however, Luciano felt it was his duty to sing in the more hallowed places of music – the Metropolitan Opera, Salzburg Festival, Covent Garden... Here he gave recitals, with piano, of Bononcini, Legrenzi, Giordani, Liszt, Respighi and others. He would also give orchestral concerts, often with famous colleagues, though he made sure they were always less famous than him.

While he was enjoying this glittering sarabande of shows against a backdrop of bodyguards, luxury private jets, five-star hotels and, alas, the passage of time, Pavarotti felt the hour had come for him to imitate the great Beniamino Gigli and choose a partner who would lighten the burden of solo concerts. We were already interspersing his numbers with overtures from operas such as *Don Pasquale, Guglielmo Tell,* and *Luisa Miller.*

His preference was for an instrumentalist. A flautist seemed best because of the spectacular display of notes the flute can produce and the wonderful fantasias that have been composed for it, most notably the brilliant, virtuoso *Carmen Fantasia*. The most eligible candidate was Giorgio Zagnoni, from Bologna, who was the principal flautist in the RAI orchestra and very highly regarded. But in the end a younger man prevailed – Andrea Griminelli, the fiancé of Luciano's eldest daughter, Lorenza (Titti), and a very fine flautist too. On top of this he was blessed with a film star's physique, which came over very nicely in the frequently televised concerts.

Thus the long-standing duo Luciano and I had formed became a stable threesome, with Andrea enlivening the atmosphere by telling jokes and teasing the members of our large troupe – there were always a few dozen technicians around to set up the seating, lighting and microphones.

A few years later we returned to Buenos Aires, not for *Bohème* but for another concert. In the meantime I had not forgotten my promise to the first violin in the Colón orchestra. I had spoken to Maestro Aldo Rocchi, who assured me that he had found a job for him as first violinist at the Teatro Verdi in Trieste. I had read about the crimes and atrocities that had been committed in Argentina – the phenomenon of the *desaparecidos* – but finally the country seemed to have been restored to normality, first under Alfonsín and then under Menem.

During one of the breaks in our rehearsals I hoped to drop in at the Colón to see some of my friends in the orchestra. I met the principal cellist in the theatre bar, and he greeted me very warmly, offering me cider and coffee. I had forgotten the name of the first violinist, so I furtively checked his visiting card in my wallet, before asking, "And our friend Munaroni? He'll be enjoying himself in Italy right now, won't he?"

His expression darkened. "Maestro, Munaroni had already booked his ticket. But two weeks before his departure…" He could hardly finish the sentence. "*Desaparecido, Señor*. He and his brother." I felt as if I had been turned to ice.

I went back and continued the rehearsal. In spite of the power of music to take one's mind off unpleasant thoughts, the disappearance of my Argentinian friend troubled me for a long time.

After the concert in Buenos Aires – another great success – Luciano decided that he wanted to visit Fitzcarraldo's legendary theatre at Manaus. Rudas arranged everything on a grand scale, hiring not just a normal steam-boat but a ship, complete with captain and crew. It was a spectacular trip.

The flautist Andrea Griminelli, Luciano Pavarotti and Leone Magiera during rehearsals in Moscow, 1997.

Andrea Griminelli, Luciano Pavarotti and Leone Magiera after the concert in Moscow in 1997.

In some places, the rivers of Argentina are about as wide as our Adriatic Sea, too wide to see to the far side. The most stunning sight was where two enormous rivers meet, the Rio de la Plata and the Rio Negro. (I hope I am not committing an enormous geographical error here by relying solely on my memory as promised.) The different-coloured waters of the two rivers intersect and intertwine for several kilometres, forming a sort of gigantic cappuccino, with natural water-displays like fireworks.

I noticed that Luciano wasn't at all interested in natural phenomena, for he merely glanced distractedly at the confluence of the two rivers. Although he was good at concealing his true intentions, great poker-player that he was, it seemed clear to me that there was only one thing that interested him about the excursion, and that was the theatre at Manaus. I felt even more certain about this when he had an argument with Rudas about not having checked whether the theatre would be free of rehearsals or performances, and whether there would be a piano available.

Anyway, after several hours' sailing, the ship tied up at a small pier in the Amazon forest, where a tiny bar served beer, cider and the inevitable Coca Cola. Luciano stepped ashore with us to stretch his legs, and an incredible thing happened: he was instantly recognised by the twenty or so Indios present, who showed their delight by dancing around him and beating drums. The one who seemed to be their leader hummed an excruciating "O sole mio". All this was so disconcerting for Luciano that at the first opportunity he slipped through a gap between the dancers and went straight back to the ship. I walked a few yards into the Amazon forest, but also retreated hastily, due to the presence of gigantic mosquitoes and the sound of menacing whistles and gurgles.

We continued towards Manaus, arriving at about six in the evening. The theatre had once been surrounded by forest, but now things were very different: it was not quite in the centre of the small town, but certainly very near it. The shacks rather than houses around it detracted considerably from its graceful nineteenth century form, so similar to the many Italian theatres that continue to make an important contribution to the artistic beauty of our cities.

When we went in, I saw that Luciano was deeply moved. Evidently Werner Herzog's film *Fitzcarraldo* had made a profound impression on him. He spent some time observing the precious marbles, the chandeliers and the frescos in this exquisite theatre. Then he ordered Thomas to track down a piano for us, and have it placed on stage. It was a painful task; apparently the theatre had not been used for some time. Finally, his trusty bodyguards discovered a dusty upright piano in the basement, which was heaved up onto the stage. I sat on a decrepit stool and played as Luciano sang one of Caruso's favourite pieces, "Ch'ella mi creda", from *La fanciulla del West*, an aria first sung by this great Neapolitan tenor.

It was wonderfully exciting to hear Pavarotti's voice in that theatre. The acoustic was perfect, and as he sang one of our group made a recording of him, which must be a unique collector's item today.

That was perhaps the only time Luciano performed on stage solely for himself, just to hear his own voice in those magical surroundings. It was a most moving experience.

THE OPEN AIR CONCERTS

As our tours came to an end, so did Griminelli's time with us. He went on to enjoy his own very successful career, both as a performer and as a recording artist.

I never understood whether it was his idea to leave us; he certainly would have had very valid reasons for doing so. Luciano always stole the limelight, whoever he performed with. I felt this too. Over the years I had turned down various tempting offers, including a contract as guest conductor with the Bonn Opera. Giancarlo Del Monaco, the Managing Director, was an old friend of mine. He was very annoyed when I refused his offer, but I could not bring myself to leave the living monument that Luciano had become, since I had contributed so much to establishing him. To this day, as I said before, I do not know whether Andrea left of his own accord or simply because Pavarotti chose to replace him with a soprano. All things considered, the decision to include a soprano rather than a flautist seemed the most logical and sensible step, since the aim was to reduce the number of arias he would need to sing.

Initially his partner was Cynthia Lawrence. We modified his programme, inserting soprano arias and ending the first half with the final scene of the first act of *Bohème* – Rodolfo's aria, Mimì's aria and the final duet – a classic for opera-lovers, and successful with less experienced audiences too. In the second half we inserted the "Duetto delle ciliegie" (Cherry Duet) from Mascagni's *L'amico Fritz*, a pleasant piece, long but not taxing for the tenor. After this, Pavarotti would end the concert beautifully with three popular songs and innumerable operatic encores.

Cynthia Lawrence made quite a statement with her forceful "big gun" of a voice. There was one serious problem, though: her Italian pronunciation was poor. She could not say "Vo'andare in Porta Rossa a comperar l'anello" (I want to go to the Red Gate to buy the ring). Instead she always said "Porta Rosa" (Pink Gate). This colour change, particularly in an aria so quintessentially Italian, Florentine in fact, as "O mio babbino caro", (which she would pronounce as "O mio bambino caro", turning her dear father into a dear baby) would drive Luciano, who was so careful about pronunciation, quite mad with anger.

After some unsatisfactory experiments with Madelyn Renée, we decided to replace Lawrence with a soprano who would satisfy all our requirements. The trouble was that the few really great sopranos were already booked up for years to come.

"Oh, for heaven's sake," Luciano exclaimed, "let's try asking Remigio. She was your pupil, wasn't she? She might at least be able to cover for the next three concerts." At that time Carmela Remigio was an up-and-coming Italian soprano, who had actually been my last pupil before I gave up teaching singing in order to be with Luciano. She was still very young, and her career was developing well.

"I think she's in Aix-en-Provence at the moment, doing Peter Brook's production of *Don Giovanni* with Abbado."

But Luciano was never one to give up easily. "Try asking anyway. After all, she won first prize in my Philadelphia Competition when she was eighteen. I'd like to sing with her, and maybe Abbado will release her at least for a bit; then we'll think about what to do next."

I was lucky. She answered at the first ring. When she heard the offer she went mad with delight. "I can't believe it! Singing with Pavarotti! I'll ask Claudio immediately; maybe he can let me go, for the next three concerts at least... that's what you need me for most, isn't it? I'm sure he'll let me."

"All right. Call us as soon as you know. And fondest wishes to Claudio from Luciano and me."

So it was that Carmela Remigio came to work with us. Unfortunately she only managed to do so occasionally, busy as she was with prior commitments. But every one of her concerts with Luciano was a memorable occasion. It was such a pleasure finally to see a soprano who could equal him in duets, with subtleties of interpretation of the highest class, to which Pavarotti, excited by performing with this extremely gifted singer, responded measure for measure, with ever new and imaginative touches, even in pieces he had sung hundreds of times.

When Remigio was absent, we alternated two other sopranos: Annalisa Raspagliosi, from Rome, an exuberant and open-hearted person, though she sometimes tended to go over the top; and Simona Todaro, from Genova, whose temperament was the complete opposite of Raspagliosi's, although her singing was always sweet and full of expression.

One day I received a call from Carmela: "I might be able to free myself for the Bucharest concert. Is Luciano still without a partner?". I contacted Thomas Reitz, who is a brilliant organiser of air travel and cast distribution.

"No problem," he replied in his hesitant Italian. "We'll send Carmela to

Bucharest and move Simona to Manchester, and there you are, everything sorted out."

If Remigio had known what would happen on the trip, she would certainly have stayed at home. It was the most terrifying journey I had been on for many years. Everything was fine going out: excellent flight on a private plane, with gourmet food. Then at Bucharest we saw a rare natural phenomenon – a total eclipse of the sun – which attracted hordes of people from all over the world, mainly Americans and Japanese. Now I knew why the cunning Rudas had arranged a concert for Luciano on that precise date – there would be no shortage of spectators.

We all watched the eclipse together, through darkened lenses. It was preceded by birds flying desperately to the sanctuary of their nests, and the howling of terrified dogs. At two in the afternoon, for a couple of minutes, the sun gave way to an enchanting starry night. The concert that evening was equally enchanting. The cosmopolitan audience was thrilled

Carmela Remigio, Luciano Pavarotti and Leone Magiera. Concert in Korea, 2003.

by Luciano and Carmela's pure voices, and there was endless applause. Luciano decided to leave Bucharest straight away, perhaps because he felt euphoric after his success.

"We'll just pack and go," he told us.

Thomas was looking worried, but it did not deter him for long. "What is it, Thomas? Anything wrong?"

"No, no. But the pilot thinks we should wait until tomorrow morning."

"Why?"

"There's the tail end of a cyclone still hovering between Romania and Italy."

"But does he think he can take off?"

"Yes, but he says there will be very strong turbulence."

"Well, if the pilot feels it's all right to leave… we're not going to be frightened by a bit of turbulence, are we?"

"Jawohl, Maestro. I'll tell him to get ready."

Carmela, who was still busy signing autographs, had not taken much notice of this conversation. She was happy to leave immediately, and phoned home for someone to come and meet us at Rimini airport.

"It's going to be quite a rough ride, you know. We'll be dancing with the clouds."

"Never mind; these things happen."

We boarded the Challenger, a small but robust twelve-seater built by Canadair Bombardier. As soon as we took off we realised this was not going to be a walk in the park. Even though the powerful engines were at full throttle, the Challenger, at an altitude of 500 metres, suddenly plunged 300 metres in a terrifying fall, leaving us breathless and petrifyingly close to the lights on the ground. It tried to gain height again – I had not taken my eyes off the luminous altimeter in front of me – but was forced down three, four, five more times. Panic broke out on board.

Edwin Tinoco, Luciano's faithful Peruvian factotum, was the first to break the silence that had gripped us. "Veronica has fainted," he announced, laconically.

The first flash of lightning narrowly missed us on the right hand side and from then on there was a never-ending avalanche of lightning flashes. I couldn't believe that none of them had struck us yet. Just then Luciano's nephew, who occasionally travelled with us, started screaming with all his might, "My ears! Oh no, oh no, it's agony! My eardrums must have burst! Help!".

You'll be waiting a good while before help comes, I thought. We could all do with some help, here.

While the plane continued to toss up and down with ever more terrifying drops into the void, then from side to side as if it was going to overturn, and the onslaught of the lightning showed no sign of abating, the *coup-de-grâce* for our nerves came from the very person who should have tried to reassure us. The German air hostess started crossing herself with large theatrical gestures, then rummaged around anxiously in one of her pockets, extracted a rosary and began a series of Ave Marias. I could feel Carmela, beside me, squeezing my arm spasmodically. I turned and saw that she was laughing, her nerves evidently shattered. I couldn't help congratulating myself just then; after the fears I'd had all those years ago, I was the only one, apart from Luciano, who was still in control. In fact even Luciano seemed to be weakening. "Well, folks, if I'm going to die I want to die eating!" he said, getting out a box of chocolate biscuits from goodness knows where, and thrusting a handful into his mouth.

That gesture, which was almost comic coming at such a dramatic moment, seemed to calm the fury of the elements. In fact we were approaching Italy, having come seriously close to crashing into the mountains of Transylvania. This the pilot confessed to us on arrival at Rimini, with some embarrassment at having agreed to take us on that nightmare ride.

THE LAST DÉBUTS

While Luciano's concert engagements were coming thick and fast, pouring money into the pockets of Tibor Rudas and Herbert Breslin as well as his own, the opera engagements were decreasing in number. Obviously there were financial issues at stake – concerts "in wide open spaces", as Rudas liked to refer to them, would earn Luciano well over ten times as much as the Metropolitan or La Scala were able to pay.

I remember another utterly extraordinary performance, so incredibly successful that if there weren't witnesses still alive today I would think I had dreamt it. This was the *Bohème* which I conducted in Hamburg, where the final applause lasted an unbelievable one hour and forty-five minutes. And that wasn't all. Before the audience of this Hanseatic city would go home we were forced to bring on a small upright piano so that I could accompany Luciano in three additional arias, a tradition from the days of Caruso and Gigli.

Il trovatore
Thinking back to the end of the Eighties, another truly amazing theatre performance worthy of his best years was *Il trovatore* at the Maggio Musicale Fiorentino. *Un ballo in maschera* and *Elisir d'amore* at the Teatro Comunale in Bologna were also excellent, but *Il trovatore* in Florence saw Pavarotti in absolutely peak form, as he had been at the time of his inaugural *Aida* at La Scala.

Much to Rudas's disappointment, Luciano gave no concerts for over a month in order to work on the role of Manrico for that prestigious Florentine performance. I was with him in New York throughout this time, in his Central Park apartment. I felt quite at home there, having spent several years there in all, including numerous Christmas holidays when Luciano used to invite me with all my family.

We went over the opera thoroughly, line by line. Luciano's voice had lost some of its suppleness, maybe through excessive use of microphones (indispensable in "wide open spaces"!). But after a few days it came back as fresh and spontaneous as ever, exactly as the role of Manrico demands – in the story he is only sixteen years old. His sticking point was the very beginning of the famous cabaletta which is usually referred to as "La pira" (the pyre) for short.

"Strange," I thought, "how most tenors worry about how to hold the C, or B natural, for as long as possible, but this fine fellow only worries about the first four bars!"

We seemed to be re-living that long gone "Chi son, chi son?" discussion from the time when we were doing *Bohème*. It was the same situation: he was apparently trying to do a crossword, and I was reading the New York edition of the *Corriere della Sera*. Suddenly he started talking to himself, which was unusual for him.

"I wonder if perhaps Rossini felt the need to write clusters of notes to create a dramatic effect – apart from *Guglielmo Tell*, of course. And this guy (obviously referring to Verdi) creates a drama with just four notes. Two of which are the same as the other two. I'm not explaining myself very well, but you know what I mean, don't you?"

The soliloquy over, he waited for my response. I looked up from my newspaper. "You must be referring to the E-F-E-F in the second bar of 'Pira'. And perhaps also the G-A-G-A in the fourth bar."

"That's right. If you think about it, there are really only two notes..."

"Yes. Repeated. You've explained it very well."

"And what I'm saying is how on earth does he manage, with only two notes, to convey everything that's going on in Manrico's soul at that moment? I still can't manage to express that as I want!"

"Try and describe to me what you'd like to express. Maybe I'll have some ideas too."

"I'd like to convey a sense of the burning heat of the flames, and Manrico's horror when he imagines his mother's charred flesh... I'd like him to have a flashback to Azucena's words in the previous Act: 'Ahi, chi mi toglie a spettacol sì orrendo'..."

"You're asking a lot from four little notes. Most tenors just bungle or gloss over them because they don't have the vocal agility."

"Ah, yes, agility, another complicating factor! But that could also signify the flickering of the flames on the pyre; then it can add horror to what the voice is saying... On the vowels, don't you think?"

"Exactly. You're reading my mind. The 'i' in the word 'pira' should have a particular colour. A colour of horror. And the whole sequence of four notes up to the final 'a' must keep that *orroroso* colour, as Karajan used to say to Corelli in his Austro-Hungarian Italian."

"Are you talking about *Trovatore* in Salzburg all those years ago?" Luciano asked.

"That's right," I said. "And how do you think Corelli used to deal with the beginning of Pira?"

"In his own way, a lot better than I'm doing. But let's not forget that he was helped by a certain Von Karajan..."

"And you've only got me to help you. But let's not forget, either, that we've both known the Maestro well and learned a lot from him; so now I'm going to sit at the piano and let's see if we can solve your problem. Should we evoke the spirit of Karajan?"

"Stop teasing. We'll get by with just his photo here on the piano."

Whether or not it was Karajan's magnetic eyes that did it (he was the only conductor we ever used to refer to simply as "Il Maestro"), within a few minutes Luciano's voice had assumed the flickering effect and the horrified tone he had been aiming at for so long.

"What do you think? Will it do?" he asked.

"Brilliantly effective. Don't forget it; always do it like this."

"No-one's going to forget it. Now let's get back to our crosswords. It seems incredible, but I can't think what the capital of Australia is. It's not Sidney, or Melbourne, or Adelaide..."

"It's Canberra, Luciano."

"Ah, good. That's another problem solved." And he was engrossed again in *Settimana Enigmistica*.

We left together for Italy, went our separate ways for a few weeks, and then, on the opening night of *Trovatore* I took my seat half-way up the stalls, one of the best places for hearing the voices, neither too far forward nor too far back. From the very beginning Luciano seemed to be in sparkling form. Zubin Mehta, a splendid figure both as a man and as a conductor (although I have some affectionate criticism of him later on) presided over the orchestra like a giant, and at the end he allowed, or rather demanded, the traditional high notes from the singers.

Antonella Banaudi, a young singer I had conducted in the finals of the Callas Competition, was a magnificent Leonora, and as for the baritone, it was fair to say that there was nothing better in the whole world than Piero Cappuccilli as Conte di Luna; but, as always, Luciano was the best of the lot.

His off-stage rendering of "Deserto sulla terra" already filled the Teatro Comunale, and when he came on stage his magnificent voice radiated into every single part of the theatre, which had far from perfect acoustics. The people of Florence had missed hearing him in a former production of *Ballo in maschera* which had been cancelled because of a long strike by the orchestra. After "Di quella pira", in which Luciano had miraculously

Orchestra rehearsal in Sydney, 2000.

managed to infuse his voice with sparks of fire, fury, scorn and horror, their acclaim seemed to go on for ever. When the performance was over I prayed that his voice would last for a long time to come. He was no longer young, but a tenor such as this should never grow old…

In the wake of *Trovatore* and *Bohème* came *Tosca* at the Opera in Rome, another great success for Luciano. His partner, Raina Kabaivanska, who had sung many operas with him, now seemed slightly more faded by comparison. Of course it was not easy for anyone to keep up with him – he was always the true hero – perhaps the great Maria Callas at her peak was the only singer who could have withstood comparison with him. What a pity it is that the two greatest singers in modern history were of different generations and never met on stage.

Just as Hannibal's soldiers became soft and unmilitary amid the luxuries of Capua, so Luciano seemed to rest on his laurels for a few years, gradually losing the fighting spirit that had always been a mark of his character. Perhaps there were health reasons for this low period. Or perhaps he was starting to feel sated by his global success, and his astronomical and wisely invested fortune… Whatever the reasons, a repeat of *La figlia del Reggimento* at the Met turned out not to be a good idea.

His voice was no longer as easy and dashing on the high notes as it had been in his youth. It had on the other hand become fuller and more powerful, allowing him to tackle Verdi's lyric-*spinto* tenor roles so triumphantly, and increasing his immense success even further. But to be honest, although he was still described by record companies and flattering journalists as "the King of the high Cs", he had not actually sung a high C for years. Now he would transpose the most difficult passages, albeit by only a semitone; only very rarely, in the reassuring company of a good soprano, would he attempt that almost unattainable note.

So I was astonished when he proudly announced that he had decided to do *La figlia del Reggimento* again in New York. Maybe he was expecting a response from me, but since he had already made up his mind and seemed very sure of himself I made no comment. Then I suddenly realised that he would certainly be singing the aria with the nine Cs one whole tone lower. This is not a well-known move; I learned it from Luis Alva when we did *Figlia del Reggimento* in Genoa. Everyone was congratulating him on his easy Cs, but he couldn't fool me, because he knew I had absolutely perfect pitch, and he showed me exactly on which beat you go down a tone.

Rehearsal in Brisbane Arena during the Australian tour in 2000.

I wondered why Luciano would want to risk cheating, even in such a small way. Did he think the American critics would fail to notice? Maybe they would, but he came down with a very bad cold, and couldn't really manage even the B flats. He therefore had to cancel, and forfeit all his performances.

At that time I had decided to resume my career as a piano soloist; I gave some concerts and recorded a CD. Consequently I had declined Luciano's invitation to help him prepare for *Don Carlos* at La Scala, knowing that he could study the part without me in New York. For once I had decided to take a break from our long-standing partnership, a kind of "marriage of artists", so that I could see to my own needs for a while. In fact, I think I was irked by the ambiguous way he had announced his intention to sing *Figlia del Reggimento* without telling me openly that he was going to sing the aria in a lower key. It was no great matter, but I disliked the pointless subterfuge, given that we had always been frank with each other, even about unpleasant things.

Don Carlos

We did meet, however, for a concert in Birmingham a few days before the start of his rehearsals at La Scala with Muti. He placed the score of *Don Carlos* on the music stand of my piano, rather shyly and reticently, as if he were about to take an exam. Sometimes we understood each other without the need for words. So I launched into the accompaniment for his part. After a few pages I stopped playing and spoke quite firmly to him. "Luciano, you're not ready. When is your first rehearsal with Muti?"

"Four days after this Birmingham concert."

"That's too little time, but if you study constantly you might just manage it. You must carry on studying throughout the rehearsal period. And then, with Muti… you know how rigorous he is, don't you?"

"Oh, good old Riccardo! He won't be too hard on me. We've had disagreements before, and if necessary we'll have a few more."

He seemed a little distant and detached. As for studying, he was not in the mood for it at all. He had been involved in other interests for some time. He had discovered *Il paroliere* ("Boggle"), a word game that might be interesting for the odd half hour, although he was obsessed with it to the point of forcing his friends, particularly Tino, to play with him for entire afternoons.

He had also become passionate about horses, and would often go to watch horse shows, especially show jumping. I don't know if he was a true expert, but he certainly spent vast sums buying colts that seemed promising to him, to the delight of the breeders who were honoured by his visits. In Birmingham, too, he bought some English horses that cost him a fortune.

After the concert I returned to Bologna. Luciano had not asked me to go to Milan, but if ever he needed help, he needed it then. Yet he seemed either resigned to his fate or gripped by a strange kind of recklessness.

I took advantage of that free time by teaching an advanced-level course at a well-known music centre in Portogruaro, with eminent teachers such as Rattalino, Vernikoff and Giuranna. I almost forgot that Luciano must have been busy with the final rehearsals of *Don Carlo*. In fact, I suddenly realised, it was already the day of the premiere. I had just got back from Portogruaro and there was half an hour to go before the performance started. I tuned in to Radio 3, which was broadcasting the performance live, and sank into an armchair, ready to listen.

The first scene went perfectly smoothly. I thought perhaps Luciano's wonderful musicality had miraculously helped him to master his role. Then I thought that Muti, La Scala's iron-willed conductor-in-residence, must have flogged him into shape, as I knew how brilliant Muti was at bringing out the best in artists.

But at the beginning of the famous duet with Elisabetta, I jumped out of my seat: Luciano had missed out four whole bars, leaving a gap which had a devastating effect on the flow of the vocal score – the orchestra was playing, but there was no tenor voice. He pick it up, with difficulty, and managed to reach the end of the long duet; but there were further hesitations, and although he reacted quickly and put them right, it was obvious to the expert ear that he was not fully in control of his part.

I felt a pang of anguish as I wondered what the dreaded audience in the gods were thinking. Luciano's uncertainty could not have gone unnoticed. If he made any more mistakes they would not let him off lightly.

Unfortunately there was another incident – a rather unpleasant-sounding one. It happened during the magnificent *Auto da fè* scene, where Don Carlos draws his sword before Philip II in a gesture of defiance against his father's authority. At a moment of great dramatic tension, he went off-key on the highest note of the score, a difficult B natural, which he quickly tried to disguise with a sob as Gigli had done before him. But at that particular moment, a sob was the very last thing one would have expected from the insolent Don Carlos.

The gallery audience, already exasperated by the tenor's musical inaccuracies, was just waiting for an excuse to explode. Its reaction was instantaneous and violent, as it always is at La Scala when celebrated singers show any sign of weakness. Luckily Verdi unleashes one of his most deafening storms of sound at that point: a clangour of trumpets, horns, trombones and drums, accompanied by a choir firing on all cylinders. The din partly drowned the remonstrations from the gallery; but the RAI microphones picked them up all too clearly.

There have always been noisy protests at La Scala, and few great singers have come through unscathed: Callas, Tebaldi, Del Monaco, Simionato, Freni, Ricciarelli… the list of exalted names is as long as Leporello's list.

This was the second time it had happened to Pavarotti. The first had been *Lucia di Lammermoor*. He now decided never to set foot again on the stage of La Scala, where he had stood triumphant so many times before. All things considered, it was a wise decision.

THE DOWNWARD SLOPE

The failure of *Don Carlos* did nothing to damage the Pavarotti myth, except among a relatively small *coterie* of exacting and knowledgeable opera-lovers.

We continued to give hugely successful concerts all over the world, in far-away places such as New Zealand (Auckland,) Korea (Seoul), Jamaica, Malaysia and Santo Domingo.

However, I could see that Luciano was not satisfied with those glories, achieved with the help of powerful and very subtle amplification. He had recovered from a period of mild depression, and I knew he was contemplating a tumultuous comeback in his natural environment – the stage of a grand theatre, without the aid of a microphone, which doesn't do much for a true lyric singer's dignity (and without which most rock singers, pop singers and so on would disappear from the scene in an instant.)

Every so often, at the most unexpected moments – in the middle of doing a crossword or playing cards – he would blurt out the name of an opera. I would think about it for a while, and when the game was over I would give him my views. We rejected several operas: *Werther*, because of his innate difficulties with the French language, and also because of the obvious discrepancy between his physique and that of Goethe's romantic hero; *Carmen* for the same reasons; *La forza del destino* because of insurmountable barriers to do with superstition. One day Luciano, who always liked to surprise people with his sudden, irrevocable decisions, announced, very firmly, a most unexpected choice: *Otello*.

"How does that seem?" he asked, in a more receptive, conversational tone of voice.

"I think there's absolutely no need to remind you that it's a well-established tradition for the Moor to be sung by heavyweight tenors, from Tamagno right up to Del Monaco."

"But Domingo is singing the role, and very well. Very differently."

"That's true. Jon Vickers and Karajan have also broken the tradition."

"And do you think that Domingo and Vickers have stronger voices than mine?"

"Not at all. But it's not a question of the power of the voice. The problem is that your voice is always beautiful. It's perfect for the lyric moments, but it might not work in the more dramatic ones, all those brutal, violent, menacing moments that the part contains."

"True. I'll try to put some 'lamp-black' into my voice, as that gallery audience in Parma asked the tenor to do, all those years ago."

"Yes, that might be the right idea. After all, the Moor also has qualities that make Desdemona fall in love with him; he's not just the roaring beast that so many great singers of the past made him out to be."

"Do I have your approval, then?"

"I hope I'm not wrong, but it's a yes."

While Luciano carried on with his game of cards (his companions Ghelfi, Bonacini and Maletti were always glad of these breaks, as they could get up and stretch their legs), I ran through the entire role in my mind.

Otello isn't a particularly high role. It doesn't go above B flat, apart from one very brief C which is more like a shout than a sung note. There's a greater risk than this, more treacherous because it's not overt – the singer might be carried away by the violence of Verdi's music and strain his voice. He needs to ration his resources expertly, a bit like a cyclist who wants to go up Mount Stelvio or Ventoux. In this respect Luciano was incomparable: beneath his easy-going temperament one would think he had a pharmacist's scales carefully concealed. I was convinced that he could manage it.

"Giorgio and I are leading by eight points. We'll carry on after dinner."

Luciano left the card table and we continued our conversation over a glass of Calvados.

"How and when will this *Otello* happen?"

"Two concert performances, one in Chicago and the other in New York. CD recording of the two live performances, mixed, plus any further corrections as necessary."

"Conductor?"

"Solti."

"The other singers?"

"Kiri Te Kanawa and Leo Nucci."

"Well then, everything's already decided. We could just as well have talked about football for half an hour instead of whether you should sing this role," I said, rather piqued.

Luciano smiled. "I haven't signed yet, because there's a very important clause missing."

"Which one?"

"That you and I live under the same roof, almost *more uxorio* – as spouses…"

"What are you saying?"

"Let me finish. I said the same roof, not the same bed."

"I should hope so!"

"…under the same roof for at least three months, so I can prepare for it. You will also have to accompany me in the rehearsals with Solti…"

"On the piano?"

"On the piano," he repeated, unperturbed, "and as my personal conductor in the two concerts and any extra recording sessions that might be needed."

"Excuse me! Isn't one conductor enough? We're talking about Sir Georg Solti, not a newcomer!"

"Come on, don't be difficult. How hard is it for you to play the odd bar to bring me in? Anyway, you'll be paid for everything."

I pricked up my ears. Falstaff says, "Gold is a good general who marches in front." So I waited to hear his terms. Since Luciano said nothing, I quoted the prophetic words of Floria Tosca: "How much?".

He took a piece of paper from his pocket and handed it to me.

"Take a look, and think about it. You can give me an answer tomorrow morning." I looked. It was an unlikely figure, which would have bought you a three-bedroom apartment in Milan or Bologna at the property prices of the day. What must Luciano's record producer have been earning? Luckily for him, the Internet was a long way off…

"Well?"

"*Venga il contratto*," I said, quoting Faust when he sells his soul to the devil. "Bring the contract!"

Luciano laughed.

"I can't reply 'It's already made', like Mephistopheles. But we'll send you the contract soon."

We finished off our Calvados with a toast to the success of *Otello*.

As we started studying *Otello* I became concerned when I realised that Luciano's memory was not as good as it had been some years ago. He found it harder than usual to remember first the words and then the notes. As for the rhythm, which had always been his weak spot, it really was a major undertaking to get this into his head. I was almost tempted to drop the whole thing, but then my cheque from the record company would have vanished into thin air! Luciano wasn't being a great help by attaching little importance to whether a quarter note was dotted or not, and whether a rest was a quarter note or a minim. Nevertheless, with persistence, he was making progress with his part, although I was still quite worried about our fast-approaching meeting with Solti for an initial "trial run" of the role.

We set off in Luciano's red Audi for Castiglioncello, the Hungarian Maestro's summer residence. He was still an excellent driver, with a very good eye for judging distances when overtaking. I was in the passenger seat; Lidia and J. were in the back. We had some difficulty finding the villa, which was set in a huge pinewood mirrored in the Tyrrhenian Sea. Once we had got through a barricade of private guards with machine guns and Alsatian dogs, we entered a small village with a few exceptionally elegant villas several hundred metres apart. Solti's villa was right in the middle of the pinewood. At the entrance we were warmly greeted by the Maestro's wife.

During our journey J. had been indulging in a little gossip, telling us that Solti's current English wife had been a very well-known television presenter, who must be about thirty years younger than her husband. He, according to J., was notorious as a *tombeur de femmes*, a Don Juan who had earned his reputation when he was conducting at Covent Garden. I added that Solti had been an exceptional pianist, outright winner of the first prize at the Geneva Competition, on a par with Arturo Benedetti Michelangeli. Anyway, we discussed him at length, and when he appeared, smiling and friendly, we all stared at him closely, except for Luciano, who had already worked with him in *Ballo in maschera*.

He was nearly seventy, but was still a handsome man; athletic, robust and energetic, with dark, penetrating, unusually intense eyes. As it was past midday, he led us into the dining room straight away, asking Luciano to supervise the cooking of the pasta.

Luciano did not need telling twice, and at once took command in the kitchen. Having prepared the sauce himself, Luciano put two kilos of pasta to boil, though there were only seven of us eating. As always, around the table we were all good friends. Wearing a tall white chef's hat for fun, Luciano brought in the pasta, which was enjoyed by all, particularly by Solti.

But then came the unavoidable moment of truth. Luciano settled onto the high stool he had brought with him, and prepared to receive – and in due course rebuff – Solti's inevitable observations on his level of preparedness. Rather wickedly for someone who had once been a pianist himself, the Maestro asked me to begin straight from the difficult triplet octaves that immediately precede the "Esultate", Otello's taxing opening lines.

I rattled them out tolerably well, considering that I hadn't yet warmed up, and on the G sharp I waited for Luciano's entry. But before he even had time to open his mouth, Solti intervened: "Not too long a pause, please; come in immediately after the G sharp. I'm beating two and I can't wait."

Luciano looked at him, perplexed – maybe he failed to understand what "beating two" meant – and did not reply.

I repeated the octaves, a little more fluidly this time, stressing the last note so Luciano would understand that he had to come in right away. He got the hint and unleashed a fabulous "Esultate" in spite of his full stomach.

"Fine," said Solti coldly. "But now don't wait too long before 'Nostra e del cielo è gloria' or before the last phrase 'Dopo l'armi lo vinse l'uragano'."

"Maestro, I hope you'll give me time to breathe, at least."

"No, you don't need to think about that, with the voice you've got. You need to convey Otello's state of mind; he announces his victory very quickly (you see how short the piece is, although it's very difficult) because he's eager to be alone with Desdemona. Do you see what I mean?"

"Absolutely, Maestro. I really appreciate your point of view on interpretation, but please bear in mind that in spite of his haste to be alone with Desdemona, the tenor is tackling one of the hardest sections in the opera, and he must have time to breathe."

"Ah, you singers are all the same. All right, let's move on."

These initial skirmishes developed into more serious clashes. Otello's second entrance, "Abbasso le spade!" was deemed to be too restrained, particularly on the C. Luciano opted for a defensive tactic. He would listen to the comments and repeat the phrase in exactly the same way as before. After a while, Solti got the message and stopped interrupting him all the time. He could also see that if we went on at this rate we would still be grappling with Act One at the end of the day.

In the third Act, however, Sir Georg produced a gadget that Luciano had probably never seen before – a tiny pocket-sized metronome. With it he checked the tempo of "Dio, mi potevi scagliar tutti i mali", and decreed that we were taking it too fast. It so happened that a few days earlier there had been a question in *Settimana Enigmistica* that had stumped Luciano.

The question was "Who invented the metronome?" and I had given him the answer instantly: Maelzel. A conversation had ensued about the usefulness of the instrument – necessary, in my opinion, at the start of one's musical studies, but practically useless once a student has graduated to advanced courses. With a slight feeling of panic, I remembered that I had quoted a famous sentence by Beethoven: "The metronome is the instrument of fools". And from the meaningful glance Luciano gave me, I could see he remembered this definition all too well. I hoped most sincerely that he would not have the cheek to quote it to Solti, who was fumbling with the pendulum.

"But Maestro, if I sing this page too slowly, the next B flats will end up *in cavalleria*."

Solti didn't understand this Italian expression, meaning "lost in the woodwork".

"What do you mean? What's *Cavalleria rusticana* got to do with this?"

"Nothing. It's just an idiom. I'm telling you again that if you go too slowly with that beating thing you're holding, I can't get to the end. Have I made myself understood?"

"But the metronome is never wrong."

"The metronome is the instrument…" He managed to stop himself just in time. "Beethoven said something to do with this but I can't remember what it was… Anyway, let's try and find an intermediate tempo that suits us both."

I breathed a sigh of relief. Maybe Solti knew the famous quote but he also chose to avoid a *casus belli*. He agreed to a compromise, cut down on his comments, and when we finally got to the end of the opera he confined himself to giving Luciano this advice, in a paternal tone: "Lots and lots more study," exactly as a teacher might say to his pupils before the summer holidays.

I left with Lidia for Chicago. On arrival, having got past the cantankerous American immigration officials, we were struck by a blast of arctic cold. Our teeth were chattering as we covered the few metres between the taxi and the hotel, which overlooked the enormous, frozen Lake Michigan, from which icy gusts of wind were blowing.

Luciano had already arrived from New York, and we found him lying in bed with a hot water bottle on his throat.

"I've already caught a cold," he grumbled. "It's as though fate is playing tricks on me; every time I come to Chicago I get ill. Do you know what the temperature is outside? Minus thirty!"

We set about helping him. J. rubbed his chest with an ointment that was very popular at that time, Vicks Vaporub, while Lidia prepared a herbal tea that she said was very effective for colds. I must already have mentioned that Luciano's colds always led to a general panic among the theatre staff. This was no exception. The telephone calls enquiring after his health came thick and fast. He enjoyed telephone calls like a child playing with a new toy, and if there was someone undesirable at the other end, he was very good at disguising his voice so he would not be recognised.

Shortly afterwards Solti knocked at the door. He seemed to know a lot about medicine, because he scrutinised Luciano intently, took his temperature and pulse, then announced, "Tomorrow you'll be ready for the rehearsals".

"I hope so, Maestro," said Luciano feebly.

"You needn't actually sing. I'll sing instead of you."

"Ah, in that case... fine. I'll do my best to be there."

The next morning Luciano declared that he felt better. We got into the enormous limousine sent by the theatre, and a few minutes later we were at the Lyric Opera. We could hear the usual sounds of the orchestra tuning their instruments, and vocalisations coming from Leo Nucci and Kiri Te Kanawa, who had recently been awarded the title "Dame of the British Empire". In the middle of the stage I noticed a strange structure vaguely like a First World War sentry box, though it could also have been mistaken for an igloo or a *trullo* from the Valley of Itria.

"What the hell is that strange building?" I asked Luciano. He gave an evil grin, like Mephistopheles.

"It's the solution the theatre engineers and I came up with, for my personal conductor."

"Should I get into it?"

"Precisely. No one will see you, and we'll only be a metre apart. Remember, don't just give me the words, but all the entries as well."

I inspected the structure. Although it was decidedly unaesthetic, the interior was rather comfortable. There was a television screen on which I could watch Solti conducting, and even a small but well-stocked fridge. There was also a good-sized music stand, on which I placed my score of *Otello*, before settling down in the comfortable armchair. A kind of sliding peep hole protected me from the eyes of the chorus – they had even thought about my privacy! Only Luciano should be within my field of vision, although I realised that Dame Kiri Te Kanawa and Leo Nucci would also be able to see me clearly.

When Leo arrived, his eyes widened with surprise. I had known him when he was still a member of the chorus at La Scala. He had a wonderful tone quality to his voice, and a very extensive range; most people considered him to be a tenor rather than the great baritone he became. But there's a big difference between Figaro and Iago, I thought to myself, as we greeted each other affectionately, having last met when we gave a recital together a few years earlier at La Scala. He asked me what I was doing in that little fortress.

"I'm here in my capacity as Pavarotti's personal conductor."

"Good gracious, what a luxury! I wonder if I'll ever be in a position to have two conductors! Maybe you could give me some of my entries too… I'm a bit unsure about the one 'L'alveo frenetico del mar sia la sua tomba'. "

"Don't worry, Leo. I'll mark it on my score right away."

I was very curious to hear his Iago, a role usually entrusted to dark voices, sometimes even to bass-baritones such as Andrea Mongelli and, currently, Ruggero Raimondi. Coupled with an Otello of Luciano's vocal quality, Nucci was undoubtedly a very apt choice, because the quality of his voice still had some lightness to it.

The protagonist arrived, wrapped in generous shawls and scarves. I felt he was making rather too much of his cold, but perhaps he needed this psychological alibi in case things didn't go completely smoothly. This début in *Otello* seemed to be frightening, even for such a great singer as Luciano; although he had rehearsed the role a great deal, he had no way of knowing how the audience would react to the innovations he had introduced.

Eventually Solti struck up the orchestra in the splendid opening pages, conducting with admirable energy and charisma, to which the great Chicago orchestra responded magnificently. Nucci started well, managing to produce those treacherous mellifluous touches that the role of Iago demands, in spite of – or perhaps because of – the lightness of his tone. I gave him the entry he had asked for, and he thanked me with a quick smile. We were nearing the "Esultate". I saw Luciano preparing for it; he didn't look as though he was getting ready to mime, and I knew immediately that he was going to sing with full voice. Solti also realised this, and didn't open his mouth to sing for him. Luciano's voice was vibrant, filling the great auditorium. He reached the high notes confidently, and let rip a dazzling B natural that made me shiver with emotion, even though Verdi writes the note as an acciaccatura, and therefore of short duration.

Instead of playing the next bars, the entire choir and orchestra started clapping furiously. Solti was a bit put out by the sudden interruption to the rehearsal, and chose to cool things down.

"Please, Luciano, don't wait too long before the first, third and fourth phrases; I'm beating two and I can't wait for you." These were the same comments he had made when we were at Castiglioncello. I could see that the titanic clash between the two of them was about to resume.

Luciano armed himself with a tactic borrowed from the footballer Nereo Rocco: he agreed to do everything the Maestro asked. But in practice he stuck firmly to his own interpretative line, until Solti, seeing that all his efforts were in vain, decided to adapt to the tenor's tempi even though he was fuming with rage.

At the end of the rehearsal Luciano was radiant. "You'll see, he'll end up following my lead. It was the same when we did *Ballo in maschera*. Little Georgie's afraid to let himself go, but if he loosens the reins a bit, and forgets his inhibitions, he could even become a good interpreter of Verdi."

I was rather shocked by that confidential use of the diminutive. He would never have used such terms about the three conductors he idolized: Abbado, Karajan and Kleiber.

As he left me on our way to our hotel rooms he said, "And from now on don't give entries to others, only to me".

What was that? A little attack of jealousy? It was so strange, it had me wondering about it for a while.

I doubt he was jealous of me – that would have been absurd, even if Luciano had claimed it – but maybe there was some old grudge between him and Nucci. Unless…

The following evening Leo was giving a lecture on *Otello* at the Italian Cultural Institute. I went along, partly out of friendship with Nucci and partly out of curiosity, to hear what an Italian opera singer had to say on a subject usually reserved for musicologists. Well, Nucci wasn't perhaps at the same level as Bortolotto or Fedele D'Amico, but he acquitted himself with distinction. He gave a harmonic analysis of several passages from the opera, cleverly pointing out that the account of Cassio's dream is introduced by nothing more than a sustained G, which is unusual for Verdi, who always precedes his arias with a short instrumental piece. Finally he drew attention to a sudden bar in 5/4 time inserted in a 4/4 context, which he described as an anticipation of Stravinsky. This may have been a slightly far-fetched claim, but I must confess that even though

I had played *Otello* many times, I had never noticed this subtle rhythmic anomaly, perhaps because the fourth and fifth quarter notes are held, and therefore somewhat *ad lib*.

I congratulated Leo most sincerely. In his youth he had been a factory worker near Milan; he was an entirely self-made man. He had not only built himself a world-class career as a singer, but he was also a very well-read musician.

When I got back to the hotel, Luciano immediately asked me about Nucci's lecture. I detected a touch of disappointment in his face as I described Leo's gifts as a public speaker. Judging from the somewhat acid comment he made when I had finished my account, I realised with surprise that he was a little envious of the baritone. Not for his voice, of course, but for the fact that there existed a singer capable of succeeding in a field where he, the great Luciano Pavarotti, had no hope of competing.

I noticed the same thing when Placido Domingo began conducting orchestras. He had never envied his great colleague as a tenor, but he did envy him as a tenor-conductor. For a while he would ask me technical questions, to see if there was any chance that he, too, might take his place on the podium. He soon realised that he had no chance at all, but whenever Domingo's conducting was mentioned, his resentment showed.

It seemed incredible. Pavarotti envious? I had never noticed it before. Yet, great though he was, he was not without a few human failings. Maybe that was why he tried his hand at painting for a few years, managing to achieve very good sales, although the art critics showed absolutely no interest in his painting.

Returning now to the tormented launch of *Otello*: in the ensuing days the battle of wills between conductor and tenor continued, to such an extent that a serious rift between the two of them threatened.

Then came the evening of the first performance. As the lights came up revealing the singers arranged on the stage, there was a moment of hilarity among the audience. Whilst all the other singers were seated on normal wooden chairs, waiting their turn to sing, Luciano was looking regal on what appeared to be *Boris Godunov*'s throne, which had evidently been brought from the Lyric Opera's scenery warehouse. I was taken aback too, for I had never seen the throne before. It seemed unlikely that Luciano had chosen it in an act of self-aggrandisement; it would have been quite out of character for him to distinguish himself from colleagues with a trick like that – especially such illustrious colleagues as Nucci and Te

Kanawa. I thought of a simpler explanation: a normal chair might have crumbled under his weight, as had in fact occurred on several occasions, including a *Bohème* at La Scala. *Boris*'s throne looked built to stand for centuries. In front of him stood a table in solid walnut, loaded like a still life by Giorgio Morandi with bottles of water, ice buckets, halved lemons and apples of different shapes and colours. His impeccable black tail-coat was overlaid with one of his famous scarves, this one a bright sky-blue, which shielded his chest and stomach and possibly played the same reassuring role as Linus's comfort-blanket.

The public's affectionate amusement – they would have put up with anything from Pavarotti, no matter how strange – soon gave way to admiration, then enthusiasm, and finally to the wildest ecstasy at Luciano's glorious performance. He had returned at last to top form with his first appearance in Verdi's great masterpiece.

I ask myself now whether *Otello* was also the great tenor's swansong. And I fear that the answer must be yes, at least as far as his theatrical career is concerned. Luciano added no new roles to his repertoire, remarkable as it undoubtedly was. His memory was already failing, which obliged him to rely on the help of a "second conductor" to feed him words and cues for his entries. Thus he began to limit himself more and more, until virtually the only opera he would perform was *Tosca*: he knew the role of Cavaradossi so well that it was practically automatic.

This was also the opera he chose for his farewell performance at the Metropolitan in New York. For it he asked me to stay with him in his Central Park apartment for about a month. He needed to go over the part every day. I did this gladly, but it was deeply painful to see him stumbling over words and sometimes even over the melody. I listened to the first performances, but hadn't the heart to attend the final one. It would have made me too sad to witness the end of his magnificent career.

I left for Italy at 7.40 in the evening, twenty minutes before he went onstage for the last time. Afterwards I heard that the audience gave him an ovation that seemed to go on for an eternity. But I hate farewells, perhaps because I am afraid of the final farewell of all, the one with no return…

MEETING PRINCESS DIANA

I had no sooner returned to Bologna than I was packing my cases for another concert tour with Luciano. This time he was off to Sweden, Norway, Denmark and Finland. He may have said farewell to opera, but his concerts continued at the usual pace; they had always been at the heart of his activities, even after *Otello*. Among many performances, I particularly remember the concert I conducted in London's Hyde Park. This also happened to be the occasion when Nicoletta Mantovani, who was to become Luciano's second wife, made her first official appearance.

On the day of the concert it rained as it only can in London. At the dress rehearsal at five that afternoon, the sky was a cataract, pouring rivers of water onto the great waterproof canopy that sheltered the orchestra from the deluge. Despite its protection the precious instruments of the Philharmonia, that magnificent symphony orchestra, were at risk from the water that managed to penetrate through microscopic gaps in the canopy. Luciano, robed and hooded like a member of the Ku Klux Klan, rehearsed indomitably, and by some miracle the sound system and lighting rig worked perfectly, unaffected by the imitation of the Universal Flood that was going on all around. We were all wondering how many people would brave the fury of the elements for this concert in Hyde Park. The promoter, Tibor Rudas, discussed the idea of postponing the concert in the hope of finding better weather at a later date. But our pessimistic thoughts took no account of the Londoners' love for Luciano. It was surely significant that the inaugural train through the Channel Tunnel had been christened "Pavarotti". And the fact is that rain, even in large quantities, makes little impression on the British people.

Anyway, for one reason or another, or most probably both, by seven o'clock an enormous crowd was starting to gather. Hundreds of thousands of people (some newspapers estimated 600,000) filled every corner of Hyde Park, leaving only a few metres for the arrival of the royal family.

Charles and Diana finally appeared, and I conducted "God Save the Queen". Then the programme began with the Intermezzo from *Cavalleria rusticana*. The piece opens with a long *pianissimo* passage, and I became aware, after a few bars, of a series of mysterious sounds behind my back. I could not make out what they were; I wanted to take a quick look, but I was already heavily involved in the *fortissimo* of the Intermezzo's

At the Savoy Hotel in London after the Hyde Park Concert in 1991. Princess Diana, Piero Cappuccilli, Adua Pavarotti, Lidia La Marca, Leone Magiera. (© Dennis Ramsky)

central section and could not afford any distractions. At the end of the piece I turned to the audience to thank them for their applause and I saw an almost incredible spectacle. The audience of 600,000 that filled Hyde Park had all closed their umbrellas, and were standing there calmly, happy to listen to a full two hours of music in the pouring rain. I was puzzled by what seemed to me a pointless act of mass stoicism, but in the interval Rudas explained what had happened: "Hyde Park is flat, and they couldn't build banked seating for such a big crowd, so the umbrellas of the royal party blocked the view of the people in the rows behind. As soon as they realised this, Charles, Diana and the rest of the party closed their umbrellas, and gradually everyone behind them did the same".

"Unbelievable!" I exclaimed, utterly amazed. "And they'll just put up with being soaked?"

Rudas smiled: "The British can take it. And a lot worse".

"I'm sure they can," I replied, thinking of Dunkirk in the last war. "But I never thought their love of music would produce such a heroic sacrifice."

"No, they love classical music. But I think this is really about Pavarotti. They don't just want to hear him, they want to see him as well."

As I walked off to my dressing room, a tiny but beautifully-appointed caravan, I reflected sadly that a scene like this would have been unthinkable in Italy, except perhaps for some great football derby or rock concert.

We opened the second half with two arias sung by Luciano: "Recondita armonia" and "Lucean le stelle". During the second one he had a moment of amnesia and I saw an expression of terror on his face. He was next to me, just a metre away, and I mouthed the words to him. He recovered at once, and finished the aria magnificently, provoking a storm of applause. But that strange loss of memory, in a piece that he had sung thousands of times, worried me. After that evening, Luciano always kept the music in front of him on a stand. He had two identical music stands, exquisitely made for him by a master craftsman in the Marche; after the concert at the Eiffel Tower in Paris he gave me one of them, which I still have in my study in Bologna. In fact the scores that he placed on his music stand were most unusual; at first sight they looked like a kind of neuma notation, of the kind used for Gregorian chant: there was no stave, only the words with dashes above them at different heights according to the melody: higher, lower or on the same line if two successive notes were the same. I admired the ingenuity of this system, which in some way made up for his inability to read from the musical stave. For example, "La donna è mobile" was set out like this:

la don-na è mo-bi-le

After the concert we were taken off to the Savoy Hotel where, in addition to the usual gala dinner, we were scheduled to meet the royals for an apéritif. Lidia and I were the first to arrive, and the first person we met in the private room at the back of the hotel was Princess Diana. Charles was not there; possibly he went off to change into dry clothes and decided not to come back. Of course malicious tongues had it that he preferred to spend the evening with Camilla rather than at a gala dinner.

Diana was well protected by a transparent raincoat which continued to drip onto the exquisite Savoy floor. Through it one could see her splendid figure. I was slightly embarrassed, as I occasionally am when I meet a particularly beautiful woman for the first time; and Diana, as well as being a princess, was truly a woman of great beauty. To make matters worse, my English has never been very good and the last thing I expected that day was to hold a conversation with Diana. I was lucky to have Lidia by my side. Her English is far better than mine, and she came gallantly to my rescue.

After a few minutes more guests arrived, among them Adua, who was not, as far as we knew, supposed to be in London at all. She was frowning and apparently somewhat nervous, so I restricted my conversation to a few idle remarks about the rain.

"How funny, here we are being just like the English and talking constantly about the weather!" She smiled feebly. It was unlike her to be nervous, but everything instantly became clear when Luciano walked in with a young girl on his arm. They seemed very intimate. The moment he saw Adua, Luciano blanched and let go of the girl.

We were invited to take our places for dinner. At the Savoy, as at all other post-concert dinners, there was a strict ceremonial to be observed: the top table, which for clarity's sake I shall call Table A, was set for around twenty guests, all super VIPs. It stood on a dais, above the other tables, which were arranged around it like the spokes of a wheel.

The guests at the other tables were not exactly ordinary folk. They had usually paid a thousand dollars just for the privilege of dining with Pavarotti. But the diners at Table A were as follows: the great tenor in the middle, with his wife sitting next to him. Then, to her right, the conductor, followed by his wife; then the soprano, the soprano's husband, and so on... all following a set of protocols which are far too complicated to explain. Luckily there were name cards set at each place, so we knew where we were supposed to sit. Otherwise confusion would have reigned among the artists.

The problem that night, and it was an enormous one, was that instead of Adua Veroni's name on the card where Luciano Pavarotti's wife should be sitting, there was the name "Nicoletta Mantovani". Of course Adua had appeared unexpectedly, throwing our party, led by Thomas Reitz, into a state of turmoil, not to say panic. The two ladies moved simultaneously towards the place of honour, *ad dexteram patris*, on Pavarotti's right. I saw Adua's face go white with rage. If princess Diana had not been sitting on Luciano's left I am quite sure she would have made an epic scene. In the circumstances, however, she preferred to withdraw most graciously, leaving the place free for her young rival.

Possibly through some mistake in the allocation of seats I found myself next to Michael Caine, who is one of my favourite actors. I had seen him mainly playing homicidal sadists and we shared a few jokes on the subject. He was delightful company, and had a good sense of humour like all good Englishmen. He asked me about the young lady sitting next to Luciano, but I had nothing to say, for the simple reason that I had no idea who she was.

As we left the table, around midnight, I went up to Luciano and could not resist an ironic comment. "Is there anything I can do to help?" I said, referring obviously to the delicate situation that had arisen.

"Yes," he said, through clenched teeth. "Go to hell!"

Adua and Nicoletta

I was fast asleep. The strain of that demanding concert – 600,000 people plus half the world's television audiences watching your every move is no joke! – had knocked me out. The Savoy bed was comfortable and, having turned out the light and shared my very brief thoughts with Lidia, who wanted to know why Charles preferred Camilla to Diana, it had taken no more than five minutes to be enjoying the sleep of the just. I cursed as the telephone rang. Like all the Savoy telephones it was extremely loud.

"Who can it be, at this time of night?" mumbled Lidia, who was also half asleep.

"Why, what time is it?"

"Two-forty. Go on, answer it! It's deafening!"

I fumbled for the receiver in the darkness. It was Luciano. "Come to my room, quickly, you and Lidia."

"Why? What's happening?"

"Quickly! I'll explain later." His tone of voice was dramatic, and the late hour of his call suggested an emergency of some kind.

I switched on the light, after groping about for it for some time. I had in fact first pressed the bell for the night-maid by mistake. I told Lidia.

"Never mind," she said. "Put on a dressing gown and let's go."

Luciano's room was on the floor above. We did not call the lift and went up on foot.

He was terribly agitated. "I'm afraid those two are tearing each other to pieces. For God's sake go and find out what's going on. Nicoletta's been in Adua's room for two hours and shows no sign of coming back. Maybe just Lidia should go?" He said this seeing that I was boldly preparing to set off too.

"You stay with me. I'm very upset and I need company."

"Right then, I'll go alone. But what am I supposed to say?"

"Check they're not killing each other."

Perplexed and unconvinced, Lidia left the room. We waited a good half hour for her to return. We were starting to worry when there was a knock on the door. It was Lidia.

"Well?" asked Luciano anxiously.

"It's not too bad. I thought I'd listen at the door, although I hate that kind of thing [and the doors at the Savoy are not exactly hermetically sealed]. I heard them having a very lively conversation, but they weren't getting physical."

"What were they saying?"

"Adua was saying, 'You'll find the age difference very hard to cope with. And Luciano's not an easy man. All that bonhomie is just on the surface. You'll regret it!'."

"What did Nicoletta say?"

"*Signora*, I've made up my mind. We're deeply in love and I've decided to go through with it, whatever the cost."

"Then what?"

"Well, you know what women are like. They said the same things all over again but in different words. Adua repeated that you're impossible when you're angry..."

I cleared my throat noisily and Luciano gave me an explosive look.

"...and then a security guard caught me listening at the door. I tried to explain – without giving names, obviously – and he listened a bit too. Then he led me to Reception where I was asked for proof of identity. So now I have to go back down there with my passport."

"Oh God, what a mess I've got myself into! The whole of London will be talking about me tomorrow."

"Don't worry. The security guard doesn't speak Italian."

"Thank heavens for that."

"So what now? Can we go back to bed, or do we have stay here for the rest of the night?"

"No, you can go. And... thank you, Lidia."

Rehearsal for the 40th Anniversary concert, Reggio Emilia, 2001.

PAVAROTTI – MAN OF MODENA
AND CITIZEN OF THE WORLD

Pavarotti's almost morbid attachment to his home town is well known. Many artists have such feelings: despite constant travels, their roots remain firm and strong. As well as a home in Modena, Luciano possessed two others of which he was particularly fond. One was a splendid 28th floor apartment with breathtaking views across New York's Central Park. This was in a luxurious condominium where Sophia Loren was a neighbour. Yet it was essentially a working residence, which Luciano used for his seasons at the Met, the theatre which he loved most and where he was most loved in return. The other, in Pesaro, was a summer home which he was rarely able to use for more than a month each year, pressed as he was by constant commitments to open air performances and recordings.

There was in fact a third home in Monte Carlo, but this was no more than a virtual residence. During his famous tax investigation, which cost him all of 12.5 million euros, Luciano was asked for his address in Monaco. He was unable to recall either the number of the house or the name of the street.

In fact, when we gave three concerts in Monte Carlo (one, with piano, a private recital for Prince Rainier and his entourage at the small Court Theatre, and two with orchestra at the Sporting Club) we always stayed at the Principality's most chic and exclusive hotel, near the Casino square. I never saw his mythical apartment, and I doubt whether Luciano himself set foot in it more than once or twice.

It may be that Luciano believed that by giving these concerts for charity, he qualified for honorary citizenship of Monaco. But his hopes were dashed by the tax inspectors, those sleuths of the financial world whose inquiries amounted in Luciano's eyes to a persecution. They decided that he must pay tax at the punitive Italian rate.

On one of those visits I made an embarrassing gaffe with Albert of Monaco. This was caused by my pathological inability to remember faces. I had been rehearsing for several hours with the orchestra at the Sporting Club when I felt an urgent need to go to the bathroom. As there were no signs anywhere, I approached a group of people who seemed to be creating flower arrangements for the tables. The man at the centre of the group looked vaguely familiar, so I made decisively for him and asked if he could direct me. I saw a slightly surprised expression cross his face, but he was exceptionally well-mannered, and accompanied me personally to the bathrooms which were a considerable distance from the orchestra pit and not at all easy to find.

That evening, after the concert, as we sat down to dinner, I realised with some shock that my courteous guide was none other than Prince Albert of Monaco. He was gently amused by the surprise and embarrassment that must have shown clearly on my face.

To return to Luciano and his relationship with his native city, it has to be said that Modena for many years failed to reciprocate the love of its "most famous son". (I use this phrase with no disrespect for the great Enzo Ferrari, a shy and reserved man who seldom appeared on TV, and whose name stands more for his magnificent red racing cars than for the man himself.)

The people of Modena tend to be closed, inexpressive types, known as the "northerners of Emilia", despite their proximity to Bologna where the

Pavarotti and Leone Magiera take a bow after a concert. (© Joanne Funakoshi)

people are more warm and outgoing. The Modenesi are descendants of the Gallic Boii, with a long tradition of ignoring the achievements of their own citizens. Ludovico Antonio Muratori, founder of modern historical scholarship on the scientific method, had been dead two hundred years before the city erected a monument to his memory, complete with an inscription referring ironically to the unusual delay in his recognition. Raimondo Montecuccoli, the famous *condottiere* who saved Vienna from the Turks, was held prisoner in Modena's Palazzo Comunale in the last years of his life, and is commemorated with a joky and irreverent memorial stone. If you ask a Modenese about Orazio Vecchi (one of the precursors of modern opera) the most they will say is that he was probably the founder of the Orazio Vecchi Music School. As for a statue – there is precious little chance of that. The same goes for Antonio Delfini, Paolo Monelli, Gino Roncaglia, and many others.

It is therefore not surprising that, as I noted in my biography of Mirella Freni (published by Ricordi), Mirella and Luciano were for many years referred to – somewhat unflatteringly – as "the two canaries". There is a double meaning here, recalling the yellow shirts of the Modena football team as well as the plaintive twittering of those friendly little birds.

Of these two great Modenese singers, Pavarotti was the one ignored most pointedly by the directors of the Teatro Comunale. Freni certainly struggled (or "sweated seven shirts" as the Italian proverb has it) to make her professional debut in her native town, but she managed it. Pavarotti had to go to the nearby city of Reggio Emilia for his first stage appearance. For many years he entered the theatre that now bears his name as an ordinary member of the chorus. Even after a major success at Covent Garden in London, and at many other theatres, his request to sing *Rigoletto* in Modena was met with a letter from the Director of the Theatre stating that he was considered insufficiently mature to be presented at the "glorious Teatro Comunale".

Then things began to change. But the lack of faith took some time to dissipate. Even the twenty-fifth anniversary of Pavarotti's debut was celebrated in conjunction with the Teatro Carlo Felice in Genoa, in a *Bohème* that later went to Peking; the major production costs (including orchestra, chorus and his favourite chef Zeffirino with refrigerators), were borne by the Genoese theatre.

It would therefore be fair to say, without fear of contradiction, that the first real tribute by Modena to its glorious son was the celebration entitled *Luciano Pavarotti: 40 years in opera* (29 April 2001). This was accompanied by a small and not very luxuriously produced book, with essays and testimonials by Rodolfo Celletti, Piero Rattalino, Giuseppe Di Stefano, the Mayor Giuliano Barbolini and all the colleagues who attended the evening, as well as Joan Sutherland, Placido Domingo, José Carreras, Gianni Raimondi, Leo Nucci, Marilyn Horne and Franco Zeffirelli.

The publication was produced by the press office of the Teatro Comunale, and of course included a tribute from I Teatri di Reggio Emilia, the city closest to Modena, which had been first to recognize the singer's extraordinary talent. After the Modena celebration, at which Luciano – perhaps with polemical intent – arranged for others to sing more than he did, he prepared a special solo recital for Reggio Emilia (at which I played the piano) with a long and varied programme of arias from both the chamber and operatic repertoires.

The great 40th Anniversary celebration in Modena was, of course, an exceptional event: an all-star concert of unusual length, requiring two conductors – myself and Eugene Kohn, a stalwart American colleague who often accompanied Pavarotti in his early recitals in the USA. Onstage were a succession of great names: Angela Georghiu, Roberto Alagna, Fiorenza Cedolins, Carmela Remigio, José Carreras, Elena Zaremba, Carol Vaness, Aprile Millo, Ruggero Raimondi and many others. Of course the Corale Rossini, the historic choral society from Modena where Pavarotti had taken his firsts steps as a singer, also performed.

Renata Scotto made a surprise appearance, thus putting an end to a long disagreement with Luciano that had begun many years before over *La Gioconda* in San Francisco. Once good friends, they had not spoken to each other for twenty years. Then they appeared on the television show *Porta a porta*, and held a public reconciliation with copious hugs and kisses, watched by a record number of viewers. Better late than never, I suppose, but what a shame it was not to see Pavarotti and Scotto on stage together for so long. He was too often partnered by singers whose Italian pronunciation was lamentably imprecise.

That same evening saw an incident with the stormy-tempered Angela Gheorgiu. As she attacked the C major ballad from *La Wally*, "O della madre mia casa gioconda", she came in a whole bar too early and started off a grotesque canon with the orchestra from which no recovery was possible. There was nothing for it but to start again. Instead of accepting responsibility for the mistake, Gheorgiu shot disapproving glances at the orchestra and its conductor Eugene Kohn. Eugene came into the dressing room which he shared with me in a thoroughly bitter state of mind after this, and it took some effort by both Luciano and me to persuade him to go on with the rest of the programme.

The Three Tenors

Whenever Luciano changed his secretary I always hoped he would find another G. I needed an assistant of her calibre in order to make him practise. But such a woman was not to be found.

It is fatal, when rehearsing, to be constantly interrupted – whether by telephone or in person – by the antiques dealer, the architect, the doctor, the notary... When you are struggling to come to terms with a key passage in Verdi's *Otello*, for instance, such distractions are not merely irritating; they actually make it impossible to do any serious work. In fact Luciano had now given up rehearsing new pieces; he was satisfied with what he had already achieved – and with good reason, for his achievements were extraordinary. But in the last few years a new idea had started to take shape. Soon the whole world would be talking about it: the Three Tenors concert.

Who first had the idea? Was it Rudas, Mario Dradi, or one of the magnificent Three? Was it Luciano himself? This has always been a mystery to me, and in some ways I am happy to let it remain a mystery, since the idea struck me from the beginning as very odd. I am not talking about it from a business angle: it generated millions of dollars. I disliked it for other reasons. First, because a whole evening devoted to a single type of voice can easily become boring – like those old records with ten versions of the same Verdi aria sung by ten different tenors.

Second, there is no music written for three tenors, except for a few pages by Rossini and the occasional piece from the baroque repertoire. None of these is suitable for Pavarotti, Domingo or Carreras.

Third, in the absence of music for three tenors, it was necessary to manipulate some of the most famous operatic arias, doing violence to composers like Verdi and Puccini (which they did), producing a musical carnage which I found truly distasteful.

Fourth and last, the bright idea of singing medleys, with one song grafted onto another, seemed to me a horrific piece of musical genetic engineering. To make my position clear, I am happy to listen to a pleasant song like *Caminito*, but when this mutates after a few bars into *Amapola*, and then again into *Brazil*, and so on until a grand finale of *Granada*, the result leaves me completely cold. It reminds me of eating an ice cream with seven or eight different flavours. That is too many – far too many – for my palate.

Countless readers will, no doubt, disagree – and I can understand their reasons. The beauty of those three voices was in itself perhaps enough of to keep an audience listening avidly for a whole evening. For me it was not so. In today's culture, more or less any arrangement of operatic arias should be acceptable, but that appalling finale of "La donna è mobile" – ...di pensier– pensier– pensier! – still makes my flesh creep. It reminds me of a scene in Federico Fellini's film *E la nave va*, where a tenor and a soprano compete to see who can reach the highest note. They use exactly the same phrase, and the effect is wonderfully comical. As for the songs, they are not Beethoven's *Ninth* or Bach's *Chaconne*, but they are lovely pieces of music and deserve to be treated with respect.

To sum up, then, I never accepted an offer to conduct the Three Tenors concert, and, because I made it clear that I would be critical – in an affectionate way – of Zubin Mehta, I make my criticism now, and I include Lorin Maazel and Jimmy Levine in what I have to say: my dear friends, illustrious colleagues, forgive my asking, but did you really

Farewell Tour 2005. Leone Magiera and Pavarotti in Sondenborg, Denmark.

need to conduct such a totally commercial concert? I admit freely that all musicians are venal – myself included. That famous phrase from *The Barber of Seville*, where the music master Don Basilio says, "Vengan denari, al resto son qua io" ("Bring the cash, I'll take care of the rest"), applies to us all. Besides, the fees for the three great conductors must have been astronomical!

I should confess that I helped Luciano rehearse the programme, even if I found it tasteless, and failed to understand his slightly infantile enthusiasm for the medleys and three-handed versions of the songs.

These versions were, I suppose, a useful discovery for the *tenorissimi*. All three were on their way, albeit gradually, towards Sunset Boulevard. With each singing one third of a piece instead of the whole thing, they reduced the challenges and difficulties, and made life easier all round – especially as the public adored what they did, and could not get enough of them.

The first concert, in Rome, was a worldwide success. I am glad I kept my opinions to myself at the time. If I had voiced them to Luciano while he was preparing for the concert, he would have teased me for years afterwards. But I did not change my mind. I continued to conduct the traditional concerts, based entirely on arias from operas. Sometimes there would be a Three Tenors event and a traditional concert in the same city at practically the same time. In Los Angeles I sat in the audience one night and watched the three stars perform together, then took the podium a few days later to conduct Luciano alone.

This was in fact the first time I had actually seen the three tenors in concert. Until then I had pointedly refused to accept the complimentary tickets that Rudas regularly offered me. But since everyone was so enthusiastic about the stage design – it was the work of an American theatre director – I allowed myself to be persuaded to go to the show. I was also curious as to why Luciano had not asked me for the kind of help that he had needed for *Otello*. I had the impression that the three tenors, once divided by normal professional rivalry, were now united like brothers in a common cause, having formed a kind of mutual support group, exchanging signals as they shared out the performance of each piece (a system which Raina Kabaivanska mockingly called "*spezzatino*", or "meat stew"). There was also a clear supervisory role for Placido Domingo, who was perfectly capable of taking my place in the slightly anomalous position of second musical director; he was now after all a highly competent conductor himself.

That day in Los Angeles my curiosity was satisfied. During the afternoon rehearsal I went onstage and stood next to Luciano for half an hour as he proudly showed me a piece of the latest technology. His music stand was not quite what it seemed. Although it looked more or less like a normal music stand, the upper part, where the sheet music normally rests, consisted of a smooth sheet of glass. This was visible to the singer but invisible to the audience. On the singer's side the words of the song appeared, three lines at a time, in large letters, with the initials of the singer's surname – P., D. or C. – marked against each. The words scrolled gradually down as the song progressed. This highly effective tele-prompter was pioneered by the three tenors. Its use quickly spread to politicians and television announcers, who could now stop glancing down to check their scripts and instead gaze straight ahead as if they were looking into the eyes of the spectators.

Luciano had also added his own private notation to the words. This system of signs, which I described earlier, was halfway between neuma notation and karaoke; it may have been unorthodox but it was also extremely helpful as an aid for his deteriorating memory.

The show I saw that night would certainly have impressed an American audience. The stage was framed by large Greek columns receding towards the back, with palm trees, rocks and streams beautifully illuminated with dancing lights that enchanted the eyes of the spectators. For me, a cynical European, this technicolour film-set struck me as the work of an imitator of Zeffirelli, but without the genius of the great Italian director. The people of Los Angeles were in ecstasies. My neighbour was highly enthusiastic, often rising to his feet to applaud. I looked at him more closely and recognised Sidney Poitier, one of my favourite actors. Although he was no longer young, and male beauty is not something I particularly respond to, I could not help admiring his fine physique and his exceptionally lively, expressive face, whose rich amber colour gave it a most appealing originality. I am not a celebrity worshipper and I prefer not to disturb the privacy of even the most public of personalities, but on that occasion I had to struggle to stop myself speaking to him and even asking for his autograph. As is my habit, however, I left him in peace, free to applaud to his heart's content.

At the Hotel Bel Air, where Rudas had kindly provided a room, it was quite normal to go into the restaurant and find Tony Curtis, Liza Minnelli, Robert De Niro and many other stars. I recognised their faces but had forgotten their names, as I am not a great cinema-goer. It would have been the ideal place for an autograph-hunter.

Farewell Tour 2005, Sondenborg. Luciano Pavarotti in his dressing room.

Our stay in Los Angeles ended at the football stadium, where Italy and Brazil were playing in the World Cup final. Several friends had flown from Italy for the occasion and we went to the stadium with flags and blue shirts and made an infernal noise in support of our team. The heat too was infernal: forty-two degrees. We had to keep pouring bottles of cold water over our heads to avoid feeling ill.

The game was evenly balanced. When Cafu, a lightning-quick young Brazilian, was brought on in the second half, Italy were forced onto the defensive for the rest of the game. Extra time was played. Then came the drama of the penalty shoot-out. Baresi and Baggio missed, and we were finished. Baresi's tears in the arms of Sacchi were unseen by Luciano, a passionate football supporter, who was hiding his own disappointment under the brim of a large panama hat.

Las Vegas and Atlantic City were the final stops on our tour. I had never been to Las Vegas before and the unbridled luxury of the hotels and the city as a whole astonished me. The façade of our hotel took the form of a gigantic marble elephant, with enormous tusks that projected several metres out in front. The lobby was a vast gaming hall, so big that you could easily get lost. It was no simple matter to find your way back to your room. In fact slot machines and other such apparatus had welcomed us from the moment we arrived; the airport was packed with one-armed bandits from the check-in desks to the exits.

I took a short tour of Las Vegas by taxi, and the sight that made the strongest impression on me was the reproduction, in amazingly accurate detail, of European cities and monuments. A great duplicate of the Eiffel Tower welcomed visitors to this fantastic quarter of town. A little further along, on the right, there was the Piazza dei Miracoli from Pisa, its leaning tower perfectly reproduced. From the taxi window I saw St Peter's, Rome, pass by, then Buckingham Palace and the Tower of London, Bellagio and Lake of Como... I was dumbfounded. But when I reached Venice, admirably copied, complete with canals and gondoliers, I succumbed for some obscure reason to an irresistible attack of laughter. This imitation of the loveliest city in the world looked to me like a parody and a joke. I asked the taxi driver to take me back to the hotel.

Then there was Atlantic City, a young rival to Las Vegas. At the far point of a long wedge of streets by the sea-shore, I saw the Taj Mahal approaching. At first I thought it a mirage. Then I realised it was our hotel, owned by Donald Trump, the celebrated billionaire.

Our concert was to be held inside this pseudo-Taj Mahal. To reach the auditorium you had to negotiate a labyrinth of gaming rooms of every kind: baccarat, blackjack, poker, etc. I have a poor sense of direction and lost my way frequently. The first time I tried to pass through, I was seized with anxiety: I was afraid I would never find my way out of that circle of hell. I asked a gambler slumped in front of a slot machine, and he showed me the way with such a desperate look that I very nearly offered him ten dollars to buy himself lunch. He looked completely broke.

The orchestras, both in Las Vegas and Atlantic City, were excellent. In a couple of days we prepared a concert with some really challenging music, especially symphonic pieces like the Intermezzo from *L'Amico Fritz*, which bristles with Italian conventions and expressivity.

I found the American orchestras highly disciplined and well prepared, even in cities like Las Vegas and Atlantic City, where one might have imagined that classical music would be suffocated by the carefree, pleasure-seeking atmosphere that prevailed.

The concert in Atlantic City was in fact one of those very rare occasions when Luciano had a vocal incident. He was struck by a sudden bout of hoarseness towards the end of the first half, just as he was starting the final duet of *Bohème* Act 1. Carmela Remigio was suddenly on her own. She had chosen this very concert to sing again with Luciano after a gap of several years.

In the second half things got worse and Luciano had to cut no less than four pieces from the programme. We made up for this as best we could, with Carmela singing two extra arias and me adding two sinfoniettas. These were all pulled out of the bag at the last minute and brilliantly played at sight by the orchestra.

Donald Trump, who had given a long and fulsome speech to his crowd of gamblers in praise of Luciano, was not at all sympathetic. He walked stony-faced into the dressing room and informed Luciano that he would not be paid because he had cut the programme. Then he made him sign an undertaking to repeat the concert in a year's time, on pain of a lawsuit for damages.

Luciano listened in stunned silence. He could not reply because his voice had failed completely. He signed the contract without objecting, and a year later we went back to perform the concert a second time. Trump was still unhappy, despite having two concerts for the price of one, because Carmela Remigio was busy in Madrid and had to be replaced by another soprano. He did not dare ask for a third concert, however, possibly because Herbert Breslin was there and criticised him harshly for his meanness, adding a solemn oath that we would never again set foot in Atlantic City – a promise that we kept rigorously and without the slightest regret.

TURNING TO POP

Nicoletta naturally played an increasingly large part in Luciano's life. Lidia and I saw her regularly and we became friends.

I was curious to find out how much she knew about music, and I took advantage of a car journey with her – she had asked me for a lift from Pesaro to Bologna – to ask a few questions. Knowledge of classical music in Italy, unlike many other European countries, is generally rather poor. Nicoletta was, however, an educated girl, well-read in Italian literature and fluent in English. She talked to me about popular singers that I had never heard of. I knew something of the work of Gianni Morandi, Lucio Battisti and De André, pleasant, amiable singer-songwriters. When she said the name Joe Cocker I thought she was talking about dogs. She was visibly shocked at my ignorance. We belonged to two different worlds.

Even if I had hoped to persuade Luciano to practise a new opera (such as Verdi's *I masnadieri*, based on Schiller's *Die Räuber*) I would soon have had to give up: our lessons were continually interrupted by the telephone, which was never unplugged, or by conversations which shattered our painfully achieved concentration.

On the other hand Luciano did rehearse, without my knowledge, *Caruso* with Lucio Dalla, and *Miserere* with Zucchero. I was astounded to hear him in those two pieces; perhaps he was ashamed to tell me what he was up to and preferred to present me with a *fait accompli*. Luciano was sometimes oddly timid about such things.

In fact he had no reason to be ashamed. They were lovely pieces, particularly *Caruso*, very well suited to his voice, and successful worldwide. Of course the partnerships were a little unusual: it would be like hearing Maurizio Pollini or Artur Rubinstein playing jazz duets with Oscar Peterson. Personally I regarded these strange experiments as no more than a pleasant distraction, and hoped they would end soon.

Since my practice sessions with Luciano had come to a virtual halt, even if our tours continued as before, I now had more time to return to my work as a solo pianist or accompanist to other singers.

In Florence I had met a young tenor, Andrea Bocelli, who was soon to win the Sanremo Festival and become very popular with a delightful repertoire of melodic songs. Bocelli amazed me with the depth of his musical and cultural knowledge. Despite being blind from a young age

Rehearsal for "Pavarotti & Friends" in 2000. Leone Magiera with Renato Zero. (© Daniele Venturelli)

he had a diploma in piano and a degree in law. He played me the first of Chopin's *Études*, Opus 10, with great skill, then gave me a lovely performance of a few operatic arias. His vocal power seemed in need of development for the operatic repertoire, however, and I advised him to work up a chamber programme. When this was ready, I promised to use my contacts to arrange some concerts. He thanked me and settled down rapidly to work. We gave a concert at the Teatro Verdi in Florence, but the place was almost empty – maybe fifty seats were occupied in the whole house.

This confirms me in my belief that he had not yet performed at Sanremo, because only a short while later, thanks to the formidable publicity machine of television, his concert at the Teatro Comunale in Modena played to a packed house. The audience were particularly enchanted by Liszt's *Sonnets by Petrarch* and Victor Hugo's poem *Oh quand je dors*, with music also by Liszt, which Bocelli ended with a splendid filato on a high G sharp; the Modena audience liked this so much they demanded an encore.

I mention Bocelli because Pavarotti also liked his voice immensely, and strongly recommended him for the recording of *Miserere*, which proved a great popular success. The two singers became close friends.

Within a few years Bocelli had become a star: in America in particular he had massive audience support and astronomic sales. In such cases one would normally expect a certain rivalry to arise. Not a bit of it. Bocelli's great intelligence, his attitude of humility and artistic admiration towards Luciano (and, I have to admit, towards me) were plain to see – no more so than at a magnificent recital that we gave at the New York Met. Andrea came to find us in the dressing rooms, and behaved like a student before his master. I much admired the way he handled himself: success had not gone to his head, he was simple and straightforward in his manners – a rare quality in artists at that level.

Meanwhile Luciano was developing a tendency that I had sensed for some time, but was now becoming more and more obvious. He began to be impressed by people who, although they had been turned into celebrities by the magic box, were really just pygmies compared to him. This tendency led us towards an irreparable clash of ideas. Even so, we continued to work together artistically with all the old intensity.

The first "Pavarotti & Friends" contained a number of popular hits, but still had an overall classical feel, with operatic pieces and a few classic Neapolitan songs. I directed only the classical part, vigorously refusing to be contaminated by other genres. Perhaps I was being snobbish. Or was I being uncomfortably reminded of that time in my youth, between the ages of seventeen and eighteen, when I had been forced to play in squalid dance halls to pay for my studies? I had done this with clenched teeth. The thought of plunging back into that repertoire, to support the tastes and ideas of a Luciano that I barely recognised any more, filled me with distaste.

Yet how could I abandon my old friend? I could see he was in difficulties with the popular repertoire, which I did not even want to teach him. One day he took me aside for a long conversation.

"Listen," he said, "I realise how uncomfortable you feel with the music I've decided to sing."

"Why risk yourself on material you don't know? It's not worthy of an artist of your calibre."

I was afraid he might be angry, but I had decided to be frank.

In fact he laughed. "Do you know how old I am? Just coming up to seventy. And these songs are much less demanding than opera."

"But your voice is still fresh. Maybe you won't be scaling Everest like you did when you were young, but you've still got plenty of puff, even at your age."

I refrained from adding that since rhythm had never been his strong point he would have considerable problems with a style where rhythm, or swing, is an absolutely essential component. Luciano seemed to read my thoughts. He sometimes had an uncanny ability to hear words that were unspoken.

"Nicoletta has introduced me to a friend, Michele Centonze. It seems he's a magician with counter-melodies, even in the wildest rhythms. He arranges songs by Dalla, Zucchero, others like that. Why don't you take a look? Your judgement is the only one that counts for me, you know that."

He was starting to flatter me and alarm bells were ringing, but I studied a few of the pieces. In fact Centonze did seem to have a remarkable gift for creating parallel melodies, quite suitable for Luciano, even in pop or rock songs.

"Very clever," I said.

Luciano was silent for a while. So was I. I had a pretty good idea what he was going to ask me – we knew each other far too well by now.

"So... how about directing the next 'Pavarotti and Friends'? You'll get a fabulous fee, like you did for *Otello*. And it'll be a lot of fun making music with those crazy guys..."

"Luciano, I've hardly ever – no, in fact I think it's never – said no to you. But this time I really must refuse. To be perfectly honest I don't feel cut out for that kind of music. If I have to do rhythm, give me Stravinsky, Prokofiev or Bartók any day."

"Is that last your last word?"

"It is."

"All right. Listen carefully. Keep that figure in mind, in fact increase it for inflation. Would you take that just to rehearse me?"

I was perplexed for a while. There was a phrase in *Falstaff* for it. I couldn't quite recall it, but the meaning was there.

"I agree," I said. "How long will it take?"

"Two months should do it. But we'll do it like before. When we did *Otello*."

"You mean *more uxorio*?"

"That's it! We'll work at Pesaro, in the house by the sea. But remember, you must help me with the performance too."

"Oh now look, that changes everything!"

"Do you want more money? Gold is a good general who marches in front!"

I smiled at the thought of the telepathy between us. We had both been thinking of the same line from *Falstaff.*

I went on. "There's just one thing I want. Not to be seen by the television cameras."

"Are you ashamed of helping me?"

"No. But I want to be thought of as a purely classical musician."

"Ok. If you really want to be incognito, we'll fix it."

So for two months I went back to a musical genre that I loathed. In my view it could not even be compared to the great classical works of musical literature. Oddly enough, everyone else was enthusiastic. I had to pretend I was enjoying it, purely for the sake of good manners. It was quite a struggle.

Ecstatic with excitement, Luciano's *masseuse* and personal assistant Veronica announced, "Gianni Morandi's coming today!" while a tiny

"Pavarotti & Friends 2001": Gianni Morandi, Luciano Pavarotti, Giancarlo Chiaramello, Leone Magiera. (© Daniele Venturelli)

voice inside me said, "Who cares?". I dislike the way these people are turned into mythic figures. They are undoubtedly highly talented, but not to my taste.

When the time came for rehearsals with the great foreign stars, the Pavarotti household went into a collective swoon. I finally met the man I had mistaken for a dog, Joe Cocker, and liked him very much. I was also most impressed with Eric Clapton, whose sense of rhythm is quite exceptional. But the excitement at the villa in Pesaro reached truly uncontrollable levels when Nicoletta, quivering with emotion, announced the arrival of Bono.

Call me ignorant if you wish, but I had never even heard of Bono. I pretended to be keen to meet him, and prepared myself for my encounter with the man who was driving Veronica and all the ladies in the house wild. I was somewhat disappointed: he was a rather insignificant-looking fellow, and unlike the others he postponed his rehearsal with Luciano until we had moved to Modena where the performance would take place.

Looking back I realise that I have mixed up several of the personalities who took part in "Pavarotti & Friends", a show that was repeated in various forms over a number of years. The shows were pretty similar, however, so it hardly matters now whether the Spice Girls were on before or after Sting, or Brian Adams, or whether Laura Pausini followed or preceded Patty Pravo.

Luciano joined in – with his own special arrangements – on practically all the guest performances. I had a difficult time teaching him the counter-melodies written by Centonze, which he often used. My task was made easier by the portable tele-prompter that I described earlier. But it was not enough for Luciano. He was new to this type of music, and he wanted me there at every recording. The problem was that the television director, deaf to my instructions, kept including me in the shots. This was, in any case, more or less inevitable, since I was at Luciano's side; I had taken up the role, once again, of personal director, as with *Otello* in Chicago. Things were further complicated by the otherwise excellent José Molina, who never managed to give Luciano clear entry signals, because he was too busy conducting the Turin orchestra; large numbers of musicians are tricky to control at the best of times, particularly if you are not used to it.

I absolutely did not wish to be on camera in that situation, and I thought of a ruse that I had always wanted to try at a fancy dress party: wearing black make-up.

It sounds easy; in fact it is surprisingly difficult. You have to burn a cork and apply the soot very thoroughly so as not to leave any white streaks or patches. I asked Lidia and my daughter Micaela to help. They thought the whole idea crazy and rather shocking, but then they found it amusing and took great care to do the job well.

A psychoanalyst might well have concluded that I had an unconscious desire to make "Pavarotti & Friends" look like a piece of carnival foolery. There could be something in that. However I set aside all personal opinions and my probably outdated musical tastes, and set off to try out my disguise.

Putting on a deep voice, I asked a policeman, "Please, where Park Novi Sad?".

He replied very courteously, "Take first road right, after traffic light. Go straight on to end. Park Novi Sad on right".

Good heavens, it worked! I had even made the policeman speak in pseudo-African.

When I reached the park I found it hard to get in, despite the free pass hanging around my neck. Eventually I explained, "Me American journalist, here for *New York Times*". They escorted me to the dressing-rooms under the stage.

Once I was in the dressing-room, however, I had to stop pretending. Thomas Reitz soon came in and told me to get out. "This is Maestro Magiera's dressing room. You can't stay here."

"Thomas, I am Maestro Magiera."

His jaw dropped open. Then he started to laugh. There was no need to explain why I had blacked up. He knew I wanted to be incognito and liked the way I had chosen to do it.

The evening began. Luciano appeared five minutes before the recording was due to start and gazed searchingly around the stage for some time without recognising me. I approached him and said casually, "Pardon me, you know where is your personal director?".

He laughed for ages, then said, "I didn't know if you were still my friend".

Concert followed concert, show followed show. On about the third in the series of "Pavarotti & Friends" – probably the one where Liza Minnelli let rip on the obligatory *New York, New York* with Luciano – an incident occurred. Just when Luciano was supposed to come in on the second verse, Liza practically hurled herself at him. Luciano, unsighted and

Rehearsal for "Pavarotti & Friends 2003". The Ave Maria: *Leone Magiera, Bono, Luciano Pavarotti. (© Daniele Venturelli)*

surprised, failed to see my signal and came in slightly late. But that was only a minor incident.

The television director, possibly unaware of what my presence meant to Pavarotti, seemed to have taken a dislike to me for my refusal to appear in shot, which involved some complicated and inconvenient manoeuvres with the cameras. Halfway through the recording he announced a break.

"How long till we start again?" I asked.

"Fifteen, twenty minutes," he replied off-handedly. "The news is on now."

Time for a coffee, I thought, and hurried off to the underground bar. As I chatted to Caterina Caselli, one of the idols of my youth, I was keeping a careful eye on the time. Exactly seven minutes had passed when I started heading back to the stage. I was thunderstruck: Luciano had already begun a duet with Biagio Antonacci. I thought I was having a bad dream. I hurried on, praying that the song would go well even without my help. But halfway through, Luciano lost it and the performance was a shambles.

Meanwhile I had returned to my post. I made my apologies to Luciano and explained the misunderstanding, which had quite possibly been intentional on the part of the director.

"No problem. The show goes out in half an hour so we can take it again."

The audience were told that the piece had to be repeated "for technical reasons", and the second time it went perfectly...

One of the last shows produced the biggest incident of all. The legendary Bono was supposed to be performing in Schubert's *Ave Maria*, accompanied by a full orchestra. But if Pavarotti was uncomfortable with pop songs, Bono was even more so with classical music, and it was impossible to make him keep time with the orchestra. Poor Molina was sweating and swearing under his breath in Spanish, showing scant respect for the sacred music.

Pavarotti signalled to me to step up to the rostrum, but I knew where the problem lay, and it was nothing to do with Molina. Luciano seemed to find it hard to believe me.

"We must get a Steinway out here at once or we're lost," I said.

"I think you're right. Can you do the accompaniment?"

"I can have a go."

I was quite sure I could do it. I am an old hand at the keyboard, and I went at it boldly. But it was not quite so easy. Bono was expressive, he sang well and imaginatively. But the classical measure does not permit much improvisation. Luciano looked on worriedly as I performed rhythmic acrobatics to keep up with Bono's voice. When we reached the end, happily without mistakes, he smiled with relief.

It was the first and last time I ever acquiesced in an act of violence to the divine music of Schubert. I did it to save a desperate situation, and I promised myself never to do it again. After the performance, Bono was particularly friendly towards me, and insisted on telling me that he thought me a great musician!

Like everything in this world "Pavarotti & Friends" finally ran out of steam. I suspect the financial losses were becoming intolerable, even for the well-stocked bank accounts of this particular host. The "friends" were not, strictly speaking, paid for their work, but they still cost money: private aircraft, special staff, cases of champagne, cars available day and night, nights at the super-luxury Hotel Baglioni in Bologna for hundreds of people... The takings were good, but they were hard hit by payments for performing rights. When RAI, the Italian state broadcaster, reduced its sponsorship, the Novi Sad Park was sadly deserted. The decision may also have been influenced by the fact that Luciano was finding it harder and harder to learn new pieces.

Towards the end of the series I managed to slip away, yielding my place joyfully to a fine young musician of the Centonze clan. Centonze himself prepared and edited a CD of songs composed specially for Luciano; *Ti adoro* was its title, but it was a not a great success, either artistically or commercially. Was it perhaps an attempted riposte to the triumph of Bocelli's latest recordings?

EPILOGUE

My relationship with Luciano was now limited once again to the big concerts with orchestra.

Harvey Goldsmith, a well-known and capable English impresario, had taken the place of Rudas; and Breslin had fired himself – perhaps he was against the pop experiment too – having written a most unflattering book about his ex-favourite. There is no doubt that Luciano's character had deteriorated in the last few years, as had his musical tastes. It was getting harder and harder even for me to conduct him with an orchestra: his lapses of memory were multiplying and making it ever more tricky to accompany him. Orchestral musicians would often lose patience with his mistakes; my friends too were becoming ever more critical of Luciano's performances, and advising me to stop working with him. And yet, despite his difficulties, I stayed with him right up to his last public performance.

He may well have been aware of his problems, because he took on fewer concerts and began to devote time to teaching. He asked me to help with this new activity, but I left him to do it on his own after a few months. He was no longer capable even of giving a lesson, and often fell asleep while his students were singing. It was all very painful and embarrassing.

Tino, his Peruvian assistant, had found an ingenious method of saving the day. The moment Luciano's eyes started to close, Tino would call his mobile phone, which he always kept by him. The ringing, which Tino set at maximum volume, would wake him up with a start. Luciano had the presence of mind to make a more or less pertinent comment on the piece he had partly listened to.

He once confused *Anna Bolena* with *Traviata*, but the youngsters who came to his lessons were very understanding and never embarrassed him. I was filled with pity to see him in such a state.

The end of his journey was approaching. He suffered from ever more piercing bouts of pain – probably signs of the terrible illness that would carry him to the grave – and was forced to move about in a wheelchair. Despite all this he was keen to take part in the opening ceremony of the Turin Winter Olympics, an event whose musical consultant, director and principal performer was Michele Centonze.

Everyone thought they were watching a live performance, but this was far from the truth. I went to Turin a few days before and recorded the accompaniment to "Nessun dorma" with the RAI orchestra and sound engineers. We had no means of knowing exactly what the singer would do, whether the tempi would be right, whether the pauses would be long or short. To be safe we recorded seven or eight different versions.

I then returned to Modena with the recordings, and Luciano chose the one that he felt best suited his voice, compromised as it was by his poor state of health.

Centonze had set up a small but very efficient recording studio next to the swimming pool. We switched on the recording of the orchestral accompaniment from Turin and Luciano launched himself into yet another performance of his signature tune.

Incredibly, his voice was practically faultless. He even found a new interpretation of the piece.

"Tu pure o principessa, nella tua fredda stanza, guardi le stelle che tremano d'amore e di speranza" ("You too, Princess, in your cold room, look at the stars which tremble with love and hope").

He sang the last word in a way that gave me the shivers. He seemed to pour into it all his most intimate and secret hopes. For a cure? No, his expressiveness seemed to point to something more unearthly, possibly a life beyond death... "Fac eas de morte transire ad vitam" ("Let them cross over from death into life"): I was reminded of those words from Verdi's *Requiem*, which Luciano had sung with unrivalled mastery.

We were sitting side by side on high stools with headphones clamped over our ears. I was directing him for the last time, making sure he was perfectly synchronised with my recording. He found the strength to go over the piece repeatedly, until he was completely satisfied. Then he collapsed into his wheelchair and closed his eyes, exhausted.

We went to Turin the day before the opening. That night we recorded the playback of the piece to synchronise the lip-movements with the music. And so, on the evening of the opening ceremony, the orchestra mimed playing, I mimed conducting, and Luciano mimed singing. The effect was superb: no one was aware of the technological trick that had been played, neither the television viewers, nor even the audience at the event, who were seated at some distance from the stage.

Thus Pavarotti's career closed with a virtual performance. It was sad but inevitable. In his poor state of health a live recital, in front of the world's television cameras, would have been too risky.

I was sure that he would now stop giving concerts. But a few days after Turin he telephoned me: "Are you free in April?".

"If you need me," I said, "I can always make myself free."

"Thank you. Nicoletta and Goldsmith say I must go to Brazil and Argentina."

"Are you sure you can manage it?"

"I don't want to let anyone down. Goldsmith has spent a lot of money organising a Farewell Tour for me. Three concerts, São Paulo, Rio de Janeiro and Buenos Aires. I would love to see those cities one more time..." His voice was tired and melancholy.

"Fine," I said. "You can count on me."

"One last thing. Please telephone Carmela and ask if she's free. It would be lovely if all three of us could work together again."

"Of course, Luciano. I'm sure she'll do everything she can to be there."

"Good. Let me know. And when are you coming to hear my pupils? They've all come on so much, and I want to fix up a concert to present them. And you must be the accompanist. Promise you'll do it?"

"I promise, Luciano."

A few days later I was swearing at the staff of the Brazilian Embassy: the last page of my passport was practically full and they refused to stamp it with their visa. There was no remedy: the Brazilian bureaucrats were even worse than the Italians.

I had to go back to Bologna and apply for a new passport. I took the train back to Milan and finally got that precious visa – in the nick of time, for I was due to leave for São Paulo the next day. I was leaving the embassy when my telephone rang.

It was Thomas Reitz from America. In a barely recognisable voice he asked me, "Have you left yet?".

"No, I'm still in Milan."

"Right then, don't go. Luciano's been diagnosed with cancer of the pancreas. I'm afraid he won't make those concerts."

"Let's hope it's only the concerts," I said bitterly. I knew that Luciano's parents, Fernando and Adele, had been struck down by that same incurable disease.

Luciano resisted gallantly and continued to give lessons for several months. He may have hoped that music would defeat his illness, but the illness proved too strong.

In his final days he was unconscious most of the time, but in his rare lucid moments he showed that he had not lost his sense of humour. He asked for a plate of *rigatoni*, and then realised that he would never be able to swallow them. He settled instead for mashed potato, and looking at me with a sad smile he said, "That's a bad sign, for me to prefer mashed potato to macaroni". And after a spoonful swallowed with difficulty he fell back into unconsciousness.

I went to see him a few days before he died. He had stopped speaking but he followed me with his eyes. When I took his hand to greet him he managed to whisper a faint "Ciao". It felt like his final farewell.

Then came that night between the 5th and 6th September 2007...

TECHNICAL APPENDIX No. 1

Basic Requirements for Vocal Study

Any young person wanting to learn to sing should possess a tone quality and an extension that are above average for his or her age (usually around 13-14, or in any case immediately after the voice has changed).

It is also very important to have a good ear for music.

No youngster intending to dedicate his or her life to music should find it difficult to sing a familiar melody by ear, without assistance of any kind.

Yet too often young candidates for conservatory study may have good vocal potential but they are incapable of decently reproducing even the simplest of tunes for an admissions exam.

These cases call for a bit of investigation: if the individual has never listened to music, it may be possible to remedy this deficiency with intensive study.

If, on the other hand, this person has had the same general exposure to radio, television, and recordings as most of his peers, it is highly unlikely that simply providing him with a teacher, a piano, and a conservatory practice room will guarantee the development of sufficient aural skills.

I highly recommend studying an instrument, preferably the piano. Indeed, if one does not have a naturally infallible ear like Pavarotti's, learning to play an instrument is indispensable; as it was for Franco Corelli, who applied himself with relentless determination for many years in order to improve his somewhat lacklustre musical gifts.

Contrary to what many voice teachers believe, belonging to a choral society or, better still, an opera chorus is not only advisable but also highly formative and educational. This is precisely where one acquires useful preliminary experience in polyphonic singing (extremely useful for ensemble pieces in opera), how to move naturally on stage, and how to interpret the conductor's gestures.

Moreover, it gives the student a chance to observe singers in major roles from only a few metres distance, an excellent position for studying their breathing and mouth formation, two of the most important basic techniques one needs to develop.

Should any of them have a sound that seems particularly beautiful and full, this kind of close observation makes it easier to learn by imitation.

TECHNICAL APPENDIX No. 2

Vocalises Used by Pola and Pavarotti

The following is a series of vocalises Arrigo Pola used when he taught Luciano Pavarotti. Pola in turn received them from Luigi Bertazzoni, who claimed they came from Enrico Caruso.

The fact that their origins go back so many years strongly supports their reputation as seemingly simple but actually very effective exercises that respond well to variation as desired.

More than one reader may wonder why singers always exercise in a major key: the reason is that, thanks to the laws of acoustics, a major triad possesses more overlapping harmonics than a minor triad and therefore produces a richer sound. From a vocal perspective this means that a major key stimulates a more sonorous response in the body's natural resonating cavities.

It therefore becomes clear why contemporary and avant-garde music is so detested by the great singers: apart the objective learning difficulties one often encounters, its dissonant nature inhibits adequate exploitation of the complete range of harmonics, often leaving the singer with a dry, arid sensation during performance.

Vocalise (1) Five-note stepwise scale in quarter notes as given here or in 8th notes, tempi ranging from Lento to Mosso; repeat as desired.

Vocalise (2) Nine-note stepwise scale, to be sung as above.

Vocalise (3) A popular variant of the nine-note scale, to be sung at a fairly brisk pace.

Regarding vocalise (3), all the protagonists in this book, from Bertazzoni to Pola, from Pavarotti to Freni, recommended maintaining the same exact position for all three *d*s marked with an x and the two intervening groups of notes on *c-b-c*. It also helps to envision the position for the following descent as the opposite of the ascending one.

This is useful training for developing an even vocal delivery, free of those annoying changes of register that Pola and Bertazzoni effectively likened to the chinking of shifting gears on a bicycle.

Keep the sound as uniform as possible throughout your entire extension, with only limited and very gradual changes when moving in one direction or the other.

Vocalise (4) Another variant of the nine-note scale, sung with the same even delivery as above.

Vocalise (5) Arpeggiated major triad, in tempi from Lento to Mosso; repeat as desired.

Vocalise (6) Arpeggiated major triad with the upper octave, in tempi from Lento to Mosso; repeat as desired.

Vocalise (7) Alternating tonic and dominant seventh arpeggios; repeat as desired.

Regarding vocalise (7), I am reminded of certain legendary moments in my studio when Freni and Pavarotti would compete by repeating this basic exercise fifteen times and more without substantially modifying the tempo (and obviously in a single breath) to train and develop the quantity and quality of their breathing.

Vocalise (8) Arpeggiated extended major triad, with the same recommendations for vocalise (3). Focus on trying to maintain one single position for the voice from the lowest to the highest notes.

Vocalise (9) To be sung the following ways:
- a) with a fermata on the highest note
- b) with a fermata on the highest note, sung *p–f–p*
- c) with a *forte* attack on the highest note, then *smorzata*
- d) quickly two or more times, with no fermata
- e) *staccato, "picchiettato"*

Vocalise (10) This vocalise, according to Bertazzoni, was used by all the greatest singers of the nineteenth century.

Vocalise (11)

Vocalise (12) Sustained notes.

Vocalise (13) Octave leaps.

Vocalise (14) This apparently absurd-sounding exercise is intended in part to relax student and teacher alike.

Its didactic principle is based on maintaining an even, uniform timbre over the closely spaced vowels I, A, and O in the names of the three cities.

We will discuss this issue in greater detail below.

Vocalise (15) Pavarotti highly recommended this exercise for developing an open and completely unfettered sound, to be rendered at full throat (including the first two short phrases, which should not be sung *piano*).

Finally, do remember that all of these vocalises are subject to transposition by semitone, working up and down through the entire extension of the voice.

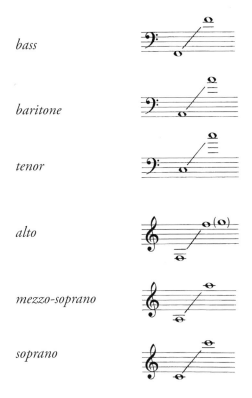

bass

baritone

tenor

alto

mezzo-soprano

soprano

TECHNICAL APPENDIX No. 3

Principles of Vocal Technique

In order to help the reader understand the specialized terminology I often need to use to describe the evolution of Luciano Pavarotti's voice, I have tried in these few pages to summarize the various issues pertaining to what Bertazzoni appropriately called the four cardinal points of singing. This technical appendix will therefore be longer and more detailed than the others.

While vocal technique may seem simple enough to the eyes of the uninitiated, it is actually constructed from a collection of extremely subtle and elusive principles. We may summarize them within four basic categories as follows: I) Breath control and support; II) Resonance cavities or resonators; III) Developing a homogeneous vocal timbre: "open" and "closed" or "covered" vowels and sounds; IV) Musical expressivity and interpretation.

I) Breath control and support

This is perhaps the most hotly debated area of vocal technique, probably dating back to the very beginning of systematic instruction. Unfortunately we cannot see the specific internal organs we use to create sound. While an instrumentalist can easily check the position of a hand, an arm, or the mouth, a singer necessarily has a rather vague, approximate idea of how the diaphragm, lungs, larynx, pharynx, and various resonance cavities in the body function. Only the mouth is viewable, obviously with the help of a mirror (an obligatory fixture of every voice studio).

We are therefore forced to work with general or loosely identifiable sensations: Who can exactly define the kind and quantity of pressure, of tension necessary for the diaphragm to properly sustain any given sound within a singer's range?

Without precise points of reference, a student lacking in natural instinct will tend to "push" too much or too little.

In the first case the sound will be harsh and grating, while in the second case it will be weak and thin. Finding precisely the right amount of pressure, of correct breath support from the diaphragm, is every singer's constant concern. This quest should be guided by the teacher, who is responsible for recognizing that exact moment at which the student, perhaps by chance and after months of thwarted attempts, finally manages to produce the right sound.

The teacher should then help the student remember the specific physical sensation of that magic moment for as long as possible, having him immediately repeat the particular vocalise or the phrase of music in the exactly the same way to perpetuate its memory in terms of the muscular tension involved.

This cause-and-effect relationship, this two-fold simultaneous search for correct breath control = beautiful sound is certainly easier for those with a good or an excellent sense of musicality, whether it be instinctive or cultivated by constantly studying and listening to good music.

In fact, when the terms are reversed – beautiful sound = correct breath control – there is also a significant incidence of success.

This idea of exchanging the two terms was quite dear to no less an illustrious teacher than Ettore Campogalliani, who rightfully maintained that thinking too much about "pushing" the breath could stifle and block the ease and spontaneity one needs to make music.

Only after a beautiful sound was obtained would Campogalliani exhort the student to reflect upon how much pressure came from the diaphragm.

This, however, is predicated upon the assumption that the student possesses the necessary musical maturity mentioned earlier: if the concept of a beautiful sound is not clear in one's mind it cannot be produced by trial and error, with no technical basis.

Such decisions are best left to the insight and experience of a qualified teacher.

I would only add one bit of advice: Do not exaggerate the kind of pressure involved *but try to adapt it to your individual vocal qualities.*

Finally, remember that the duration of a breath is determined more by how slowly and gradually one exhales than by the quantity of air one inhales.

Teachers already understood long ago that the flame of a candle placed before a singer's mouth should not waver with his breath. This means that the utmost care must be taken to keep the diaphragm as steady as possible once the correct degree of pressure is established, so that this ideal position can render the best results with the least effort.

We will return to this monumentally important issue when discussing the encounter between Pavarotti and Sutherland.

II) Resonance cavities or resonators

When a column of air issuing from the lungs is projected upward by the relaxing muscle of the diaphragm, at a certain point in its path it encounters two thin elastic bands of muscle tissue located in the larynx and sets them in vibration. These are the vocal cords, the origins of the human voice.

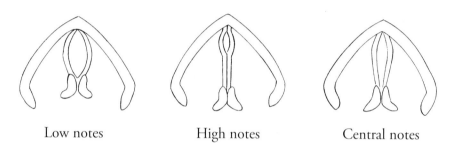

Low notes   High notes   Central notes

A veil of mystery surrounds the vocal cords. One would presume that an expert ear-nose-and-throat physician/otolaryngologist could easily identify any type of voice from a laryngoscopic exam, but this is often not the case; indeed, it would even appear that there is no appreciable difference between the vocal cords of a famous singer and those of someone who has given no thought whatsoever to taking up such activity.

Experiments of a rather macabre nature performed on the vocal cords of cadavers have demonstrated that when these organs vibrate they actually produce an extremely faint sound.

What then is the source of power in a great operatic voice? The phenomenon may be compared to what happens in a Stradivari or Guarneri del Gesù violin or a fine piano.

The weak initial sound of the strings is amplified to incredible proportions by the resonating chamber of the instrument; the larger and more harmoniously proportioned these instruments are, the richer and more powerful the sound.

The principal resonance cavities (or resonators) of the human body are, from the lowest regions upward: first of all the chest (which some researchers believe to be insignificant), the larynx, the pharynx, the mouth, the nose, and other cranial cavities, particularly the nasal cavities behind the nostrils and the frontal sinuses.

It is fairly clear that many of these cavities are fixed and unchangeable entities that cannot be expanded even with the most assiduous study: in other words, if you have an underdeveloped palatal arch or a small mouth, there is no choice but to accept what Mother Nature has given you.

On the other hand, what can be improved with study is how the column of air is projected, particularly toward the soft palate to stimulate the upper resonance cavities, the famous "mask" that, as Eugenio Montale so cleverly observed, every singer cultivates with the passion of a great cook blending and whisking his mayonnaise.

The conquest of a satisfying sound can also be achieved by adapting the earlier equation regarding respiration to read thus: correct mouth aperture = correct sound, and exchanging the terms as explained above.

Certainly the mouth is the most important resonator, especially because it functions as the exit point for the flow of sound.

Maximum attention should therefore be devoted to the correct mouth aperture, as Pavarotti himself confirmed on the cd-rom *Scuola di Canto Freni-Pavarotti*.

The best aperture is a vertical one, more or less like a yawn, completely free of tension.

Once this basic principle has been established, however, exactly what is the correct size of aperture for the multitude of sounds and dynamics in any given piece of music?

Here again, as in breathing technique, the student must rely upon his individual artistic sensitivity and his teacher's experienced ears.

It may seem at times that the difficulties one faces in this enterprise are all but impossible to overcome. Regulating the mouth aperture contemporaneously involves sonorizing the upper resonance cavities as well, specifically the nose (but without creating a nasal sound!), the nasal cavities, and the frontal sinuses.

In other words, the entire upper region of the body should become one harmonious and powerful resonance chamber.

Unfortunately these phenomena are not possible to see, and the ear, which is ill-situated for providing an accurate impression of one's own voice, is of little help for correcting faulty projection.

The student must therefore rely upon remembering those particular inner sensations that coincide with what the teacher identifies as the right sound.

This spasmodic search for the ideal sound, rather like the "blue note" of Chopin fame, is necessarily relentless but also extremely stimulating work.

In summary, then, we may observe that the two issues of greatest concern for a singer involve supporting the voice from the diaphragm (or modulating the air pressure) and successfully engaging the proper resonators for one's particular vocal qualities.

They may be subject to unpredictable variables: a simple upset stomach can substantially disturb one's breathing, or a cold might block some of the resonating cavities. When this occurs the singer must rely upon his skill and composure to offset the difficulty by changing his way of breathing or by obtaining still more from those resonating cavities that are not obstructed.

Even advancing age and the choice of repertoire may make it necessary to modify the way the diaphragm and the resonators are used.

It was this ongoing task that the famous Beniamino Gigli, at over sixty years of age, would pursue in his dressing room at the Teatro Comunale in Modena while a young Luciano waited patiently to be able to speak with him; and it was the same task that this lad, destined to become perhaps even more famous than Gigli, would also come to pursue every day of his life with constant and contemplative care.

III) Developing a homogeneous vocal timbre; "open" and "closed" or "covered" vowels and sounds

Just as every instrument possesses a homogeneous timbre, a particular sound that can be immediately recognized for its individual tone qualities, so too the singer needs to develop uniformity and personality in his sound.

This involves:

a) Converging vowel colours;

b) rounding and gracefully negotiating the awkward leaps often encountered in moving from one register to another.

A) CONVERGING VOWEL COLOURS

Vowels are usually categorized as bright or dark. The bright vowels are I and E while O and U are dark, with A lying between them.

Light vowels   Dark vowels
   I E ⟶ A ⟵ O U

To obtain an even, uniform sound it is necessary to merge the two opposing groups of vowels, ideally by following the arrows indicated above.

This means that the bright vowels are sung darker and the dark vowels brighter. Similar suggestions appear in many authoritative singing treatises, although there is no attempt to explain what precise gradation, what exact mixture of sound colour they might recommend.

This is a difficult obstacle for the aspiring singer to overcome, but one which we may nonetheless address with the following advice.

It may be observed that in singing the brightest vowels, particularly in the zones of transition, the sound loses its focus and becomes throaty and coarse (in technical jargon we call it "squeezed").

Opportunely and subtly darkening the sound as described above – which can be facilitated, while singing I, E, and A, by imagining the sound of the French word "fleur", or the U as it is pronounced in Lombard dialect – makes it possible to recuperate the "mask" resonance quickly. Others find it preferable to think of a dark O or even a dark U when enunciating a bright vowel. These devices also help resolve many of the problems discussed in the following section.

B) VOICE BREAKS ACROSS CHANGES OF REGISTER

Let us consider for a moment the changes of register for the tenor voice. From low C to fourth-space treble E-flat, vowel enunciation may be brighter and more open. From E-flat on upwards it should begin to darken ("close" or "cover" in technical jargon) the bright vowel timbre. This does not mean that the voice will be less sonorous: on the contrary, singing in the "mask" prevents the voice from falling into the throat and facilitates emission, thus proving advantageous for sound quality and less demanding on the vocal cords.

Not everyone endorses this technique for changing register. Some purists, like Gianandrea Gavazzeni, do not tolerate what they consider a corruption of the Italian language, an assault on its correct pronunciation. Such opinions are more than justifiable from a theoretical point of view.

From a practical one, however, nearly all voices that do not use this covered-sound technique end up ruined after only a few years.

The most notorious example of this kind of premature deterioration was the tenor Giuseppe Di Stefano, who was blessed with a naturally and incomparably beautiful voice.

Di Stefano had the good (or bad!) fortune to possess a rare gift: a lovely open quality over precisely that change of register where other tenors are obliged to darken their vowels and cover them in order to avoid sounding throaty and compressed.

The abuse of open sounds soon proved disastrous for Di Stefano: the first sign of trouble was the increasing difficulty he encountered in reaching his high notes, then his entire extension began to suffer; beautiful sounds they were indeed, but he produced them by singing "on the vocal cords" and not in the mask.

He was therefore ever more frequently forced to give up concerts dramatically and without warning because his voice had just as suddenly dropped. The premature retirement of this great tenor from the operatic stage continues to be mourned by those who can never forget his beautiful timbre, captivatingly incisive phrasing, and extraordinary artistry.

Pavarotti, who steadfastly admired and studied Di Stefano's interpretive example, nonetheless never surrendered to the temptation of regularly singing open vowels over a change of register: he too possessed this natural gift but he would use it sparingly, for a particular expressive effect.

Unlike Di Stefano's approach, his technique for covered singing was truly a textbook standard. Having learned it from Arrigo Pola (who, as we know, learned it in turn from Luigi Bertazzoni based on the legacy of Enrico Caruso), with an attentive ear to the contemporary examples of Carlo Bergonzi and, even more so, Gianni Raimondi (an absolute fanatic for covered sound), Pavarotti was admirably able to "cover" the entire area of his change of register without giving the impression that he had overly compromised an accurate rendition of the bright vowels.

Among those of his generation, his diction was rivaled by none; among the great voices of the past, only Tito Schipa, Aureliano Pertile, and (with the aforementioned technical reservations) Giuseppe Di Stefano could boast the same clarity and precision of pronunciation.

Table of the areas for each vocal range
where the change of register occurs

Tenor and soprano

Mezzo-soprano and baritone

Alto and bass

IV) Musical expressivity and interpretation

I will limit myself in this most important and seemingly endless expanse of a young person's artistic preparation to the exposition of four rules. They are rarely addressed clearly in vocal treatises and only the great interpreters put them to constant use.

1) *Exploit the dynamics as much as possible.* A singer who understands how to apply dynamic colour is able to both engage and maintain the interest of the listener.

The classic crescendo and diminuendo need not be restricted to long phrases alone: groups of three or two notes, or even one note, can seem more luminous and expressive with an able touch of dynamic colour.

2) *As the melodic line rises, accompany it with a crescendo; in its descent, with a diminuendo.*

Remember that the composer can go into only so much detail: were it necessary to indicate all the expressive colours to use the stave would not be able to contain them.

Therefore do not hesitate to add as much dynamic and expressive color as possible, obviously remaining within the limits of good taste.

3) As a consequence of the previous point: *The highest note of a phrase is almost always the most expressive one.*

Do not fail to highlight it in some way, perhaps "lingering" on it just enough to distinguish the artist from the simple singer.

4) *Always remember that your voice reflects how you feel.* If you are sad your voice will seem melancholy, if you are happy it too will ring cheerful. Therefore you should try to assume the emotional state of the character you interpret and to express all the nuances of the text, just as great actors do.

Given that the current trend is not to learn an entire opera at the outset but to begin only with the more famous arias, I would highly recommend taking the time to develop a broader perspective of the complete character. This will make it easier to capture the expressive essence of even a single piece.

Consider one famous example: "Mi chiamano Mimì".

If the soprano concentrates on studying this aria alone she may well be unaware of one fundamental element: that the protagonist is suffering from tuberculosis. A soprano who does not take this into account would likely be completely mistaken in her interpretation, quite possibly singing the entire piece in full force, with a healthy, robust voice.

Instead it is necessary to research and reflect upon the hypersensitivity of those stricken with this disease, upon their yearning for life and for love; this makes for a better understanding of the genius of Puccini's music in this splendid aria, with its sudden bursts of energy alternating with moments of listless abandon.

Once this is done it will be easier to find the right shade, the most appropriate vocal colour for portraying her particular character.

Interpretation is an increasingly important factor in a singer's development. With the established dominion of great conductors and the consequent refinement of public taste, no singer can simply get by with a beautiful, booming voice. One must therefore undertake from the very start not only the pursuit of technical progress but also the development of a sense of musicality, which includes such elements as rhythm, phrasing, legato, expressivity, and intonation.

Musical Expressivity at the Service of Technique

Campogalliani, as we have seen, wasted little time analyzing technical problems. Yet he did not ignore them: he simply tended to solve them by encouraging the student to seek the most appropriate sound for a particular dramatic and musical situation.

His approach to improving the way his students sang was to work with them on a psychological level: as when he advised Pavarotti to put aside his technical concerns regarding the beginning of "Che gelida manina" and to concentrate only on imagining the character's state of mind.

It was then that the young tenor discovered the effectiveness of a particular kind of sound called soffiato or *soufflé* or "breathy", which is obtained by filling the throat and the "mask" with air while making the vocal chords vibrate as little as possible. Two excellent examples of this are the way Pavarotti sang certain phrases in the finale of *Un ballo in maschera* ("Ella è pura, in braccio a morte") and his best entrances for "Una furtiva lacrima".

There were other technical results and improvements that Pavarotti would discover alone, but always along this same path indicated by Campogalliani: that is, in the continuous search for solutions in terms of musical expressivity.

For example, he came to realize that his entrance on that difficult opening F in "Una furtiva lacrima" was far more successful when he would assume an expression of surprise. His advice to a student who asked him how he created that marvellous sound was: "Look astonished"; and the student did not understand, imagining that the Maestro was joking or being eccentric without even remotely realizing that the expression on his own face at that instant would probably have been just right for the sound he sought.

Sometimes very little is needed, perhaps no more than a slight variation in the facial muscles, the mouth aperture, or the way the lips are set to obtain seemingly impossible success.

For a long time during his younger years Pavarotti worked at another kind of sound that caught his imagination, one that Di Stefano often used (especially in the first octave and a half of his extension) and curiously enough also Tony Dallara, a very popular non-classical singer at the time. He was finally able to uncover the secret: by imagining a slight closing of the nasal cavities he could engage the particular physical mechanism he needed, after which he adapted it to his own voice and temperament with excellent results.

Campogalliani rarely had his students sing more than ten minutes of vocalises. The exercises he generally used were the ones by Bertazzoni and Pola, which were inherited from Rosina Storchio; but he often varied them because he believed that the student should always be kept on his toes, and he required that they be sung on all the vowels but U. Having himself theorized the concept of converging vowels, he would never allow them to sound too bright and tight, particularly the I and E, preferring that they all possess a homogeneous timbre.

His favorite vocalises were the following:

THE IMPORTANCE OF MEDICAL CHECKS

If a singer is troubled by a disorder that persists over a period of time, as the young Pavarotti was, it is essential to consult a doctor. However, singers may also experience other, more fleeting and insidious problems, which may not seem to require a visit to a specialist. Quite often a young, inexperienced singer can over-exert the vocal cords. Robust as these are, they cannot be mistreated with impunity. If they become even slightly reddened and inflamed, they must be rested for a few days. If one continues to sing and, even worse, to force the voice, the inflammation can quickly develop into something much more serious – the dreaded nodule, which diminishes the elasticity and power of the vocal cords. As long as the nodule is diagnosed early enough by a specialist, it can be reabsorbed after a period of rest, which in some cases needs to last several months. If the advice is ignored, and one foolishly continues to sing, there can be irreversible damage to the singing voice and even to the speaking voice. Therefore, at the first signs of abnormal vocal fatigue, a singer should consult a specialist and undergo a laryngoscopy.

In order to keep the vocal cords healthy, the following rules should be adhered to, especially in the early years of a singer's career.

1. *Do not practise for more than an hour and a half a day, broken into shorter sessions.*
2. *Do not exceed four days of practice a week.*
3. *Do not sing for too long in the high register.*
4. *Do not strain the voice. Re-read the technical appendix on the subject of breath control and the resonance cavities or resonators; the correct breath support and choice of resonators will prevent damage to the vocal cords.*

It is essential to respect these four rules. The young student should not lend too much credence to certain interviews in which famous singers claim to devote their entire day to voice exercises. In fact, all the great singers that I have known are very careful not to subject their vocal cords to excessive strain, since these are the most vulnerable parts of the phonatory system.

From what I have been told by those who were artistically very close to Maria Callas, I have good reason to suspect that her premature vocal decline might actually have been caused by excessive practising. It seems that this superb Greek singer did far too much voice training – as much as eight hours a day, split between *solfèges* (she favoured Giuseppe Concone's *50 Lessons*), vocalises, and going over vocal scores. It seems reasonable, therefore, to wonder whether this incessant quest for perfection might not have worn out her larynx prematurely, even though her sudden, mysterious vocal decline is commonly attributed to her rapid weight loss.

5. *Do not sing if you are unwell or if you have a cold. Only an expert singer can hope to get by under conditions of such discomfort.*

It is worth remembering that maintaining one's vocal health is even more important than a début in a famous theatre. Another example from Maria Callas, this time a positive one, applies to all singers: due to ill-health she wisely cancelled her performances in *Norma* at the Rome Opera, bravely facing up to the inevitable attacks from the press, and the subsequent court case, which she won.

Like athletes, singers should lead a healthy life. Diet and physical exercise should be well-balanced and free from excesses. As for their sex life, there is some disagreement over this.

Until quite recently it was thought that female singers could carry on their sex lives as usual, and even that sexual intercourse shortly before a performance was beneficial for sopranos and mezzosopranos. Singing teachers in the past also ruled that low voice male singers could lead a more or less normal sex life. Tenors, however, had to endure long abstinences. According to Antonio Melandri, tenors should avoid intercourse from the first day of rehearsals until the last performance. His pupil Gianni Raimondi objected to this strict regime; he had been signed up at a very young age by Carlo Alberto Cappelli on twelve-month contracts, and, as he told his inflexible teacher, he refused to make a vow of chastity for 365 days a year...

More recently, sexologists have repudiated such absurd beliefs, and have established that sexual activity can even be beneficial for singers, as for athletes, if practised sensibly and in accordance with one's needs, which vary from one individual to another.

TECHNICAL APPENDIX No. 5

The Audition

The audition, that strange ritual of evaluating a singer by having him or her pretend to engage an empty, cold and lifeless hall with the doubtful assistance of a frequently inexperienced accompanist, is a decidedly superficial means of pronouncing lapidary judgment on a young artist's future.

Countless cases of outrageous errors, often not far short of the ridiculous, lie documented in theatrical archives: like those of Mirella Freni at Bologna or Lucia Valentini Terrani at La Scala, both hopeful young candidates whose voices were deemed to lack projection and who would, in the opinion of their hasty examiners (who out of charity shall be maneless), undoubtedly never enjoy a professional career.

On the other hand, no one to date has been able to come up with an alternative evaluation procedure that is equally rapid and efficient.

It is therefore absolutely necessary that a young singer begin to develop the psychological means to overcome the problems that this kind of challenge entails.

The principal difficulties are three:

1) *Performing without an audience.* This may inhibit the desire to communicate, to find the emotional energy necessary to successfully release one's full powers of expression.

The only solution I can suggest is to exploit the imagination as a means of psychological motivation. Remember that the context is more or less the same as a recording studio, although at least in the latter case the presence of an orchestra and chorus tends to serve as a kind of emotional sounding board.

2) *Choice of repertoire.* It is of paramount importance to choose arias that best demonstrate your ability and potential.

Since almost no one asks for more than one or at best two pieces for a total duration of 3-8 minutes (the audition with Gavazzeni described earlier is by no means the norm!), you must absolutely be able to showcase your best qualities within this fleeting moment, one that may well decide your destiny. Maximum attention therefore regarding the music you choose.

3) *The accompanist.* As I have said, it is becoming increasingly difficult for theatres to find good accompanists. Whenever possible the singer should bring his own if the pianist is suitably tried and true. Otherwise try to explain your ideas of interpretation and tempo to the accompanist before hand.

Often I am asked: How does one go about getting an audition?

Sometimes it is not as difficult as it may seem. If you are not under the management of an agent, simply write a registered letter to the artistic director of the theatre, briefly describing your type of voice and repertoire and including a concisely formulated curriculum if you have one.

Since the theatres in Italy are public entities they are obliged to answer within a reasonable period of time; should that not occur, however, it is reasonable to solicit a response with a follow-through telephone call. In extreme cases even a letter from your lawyer can stir a distracted or negligent administrator to action.

There is also a certain strategy, a simple tactic that can considerably shorten this waiting period.

Try to discover in advance what operas have been programmed for the upcoming season of the theatre where you want to audition, as often as not simply by consulting the theatre's publicity material. This allows you to be able to focus your preparation on one or two titles, choosing your audition arias accordingly and declaring both in your written request and at the audition that you have the entire role in your repertoire.

This declaration, supported by fact of course (and a successful audition), assures you the substantial possibility of being called in to substitute on short notice if, as often happens, the singer already engaged for the role becomes ill or indisposed.

It is much more unlikely that the theatre would remember even the most brilliant auditions after a few years and with no direct relevance to the season at hand.

One should also remember that when it comes to choosing singers, the weight of authority and decisional autonomy of an important conductor are second to precious few in the theatre, including even such a famous and prestigious artistic director as was Francesco Siciliani. The conductor's approval is therefore indispensable for an artist's stage debut.

An audition with someone like Abbado, Muti, or Chailly can have far more impact than a long string of auditions with artistic directors or secretaries who are often incompetent and at their worst inclined to be arrogant in order to disguise the fact that they actually have no decision-making power whatsoever.

TECHNICAL APPENDIX No. 6

Vocal Style in the Epoch of Mozart

Trying to define style is an arduous task indeed.

We often say that someone "has style". Yet it is anything but simple to analyse the delicate nuances of this characteristic, to understand its rather elusive and mysterious nature.

The same is true for vocal styles. Every epoch, every composer, every musical work has an individual style that the interpreter needs to understand. For Mozart we can identify at least two very distinct stylistic features: elegance and lightness.

In terms of vocal technique, they require certain specific expedients. The emission should be responsive and quick, always projected into the upper zone of the "mask"; in technical jargon we call this "cantare di punta", which produces a more brilliant, agile sound. Portamento should be all but completely eliminated, and any Romantic or Verist kind of dramatic emphasis is absolutely out of the question. Take care, however, not to err in the opposite direction by stripping away all expressivity. Mozart's music is no less subject to the standard rules of phrasing and dynamics than any other. Vibrato should be used, if with discretion; otherwise the absence of vibrato produces that characteristic and unpleasant train-whistle kind of sound which is typical of many raised in the German school of singing.

When Pavarotti turned to the music of Mozart it had a beneficial effect on his voice, forcing him to sharpen the focus of his sound after it had been "stretched" too much in that period from so many performances of *La bohème*.

But exclusive and extended dedication to this repertoire can also create serious consequences for:

– the full physical resonance spectrum, since the upper resonance cavities are privileged;

– complete and continuous breathing resources, given that the character and style of this composer do not require the same kind of exaggerated breathing one encounters instead in the Romantic and Verist repertoire.

It is therefore good for the young singer to gradually investigate all styles and emission techniques without falling prisoner to any one in particular, unless evident physical limitations suggest concentrating on a specialized repertoire. In that case early music, lieder, or contemporary music, for example, are genres in which intelligence and musicality carry more weight than the presence of raw natural talent.

TECHNICAL APPENDIX No. 7

Breathing Techniques

I have already addressed some of the problems regarding this aspect of vocal technique in Technical Appendix No. 3.

Given its importance, however, I would like to return to this issue here in more detail by focusing on the basic anatomical and physiological principles involved and illustrating the current major schools of thought.

The respiratory system consists of:

LUNGS
Residing within the chest cavity and surrounded by the rib cage, they require the thorax to expand as they fill with air (inhalation); and in the opposite process they return to their original size as the thorax contracts (exhalation).

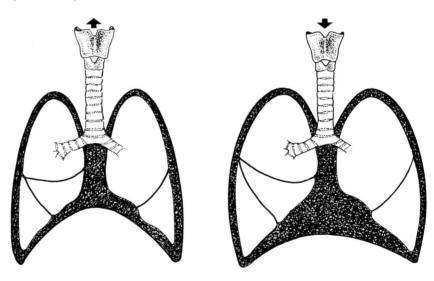

THORACIC (RIB) CAGE
This is the collection of paired ribs attached to the sternum on the chest and to the spinal column on the back.

Expansion of the rib cage is possible thanks to the intercostal muscles, which when activated raise the upper ribs and widen the lower ones.

If the upper ribs are raised the breathing is called costal; while the widening of the lower ribs, which involves abdominal expansion by flexing the diaphragm, is called diaphragmatic breathing.

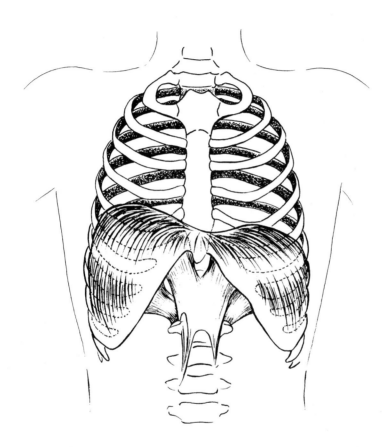

DIAPHRAGM

This is a strong, dome-shaped sheet of muscle and tendon that separates the thoracic cavity from the abdominal cavity. It lies beneath the lungs, and when lowered by contraction it provides more space for them to expand with air (inhalation).

As it relaxes the abdominal muscles help by compressing the abdominal organs, forcing the air to escape from the lungs (exhalation).

ABDOMINAL MUSCLES

The abdominal muscles are the observable part of our respiratory system.

For this reason, when breathing is approached in terms of singing, the abdominal wall should be attentively examined both visually and manually. In fact, for diaphragmatic breathing it expands outward during inhalation and contracts during exhalation. Often this area is incorrectly called the diaphragm in the approximate terminology of many teachers, students, and enthusiasts.

While nearly all voice teachers are agreed that diaphragmatic inhalation is most preferable (as the best normal way to take in the most air in only fractions of seconds), breath support for singing (exhalation) is still an area of controversy.

There are four basic schools of thought:

The first, originally theorized by Bertazzoni and subsequently by his student Pola, favors a slow emission of air by contracting the abdominal muscles and consequently compressing the abdomen.

The second, on the other hand, favors relaxing the abdominal muscles, which consequently causes the abdomen to expand.

The third, which has been attributed to Joan Sutherland by Freni and Pavarotti, is mixed breath support. The sensation should be similar to what one feels when trying to imitate the sound of a squealing newborn, as Pavarotti explained on the cd-rom *Scuola di Canto Freni-Pavarotti*.

The fourth, which was used for example by Sesto Bruscantini, advocates imagining diaphragmatic support that draws on tension in the posterior thoracic and even the gluteous muscles.

At the cost of sounding repetitive I want to remind the reader that muscular tension should always remain elastic: too much tension creates harsh and awkward sounds. The entire upper region of the body should be thoroughly relaxed and the throat wide open. To achieve this Pavarotti would say that the sound begins in the throat and has to fill it completely.

Actually sound begins in the larynx; but since it is impossible to have such precise physical sensations, speaking generically of the throat is certainly effective. Be careful, however, not to confuse this with the feeling of a throaty sound, which is one of the worst defects in singing.

Since it is very difficult to have a clear grasp of all the parts of the body that are involved in breathing, the singer often relies upon mental images for physical sensations (support from the kidneys, support from the diaphragm expanding outward, contracting inward or downward) that are very imprecise because they do not always correspond to the physiological mechanism involved, but they are sometimes an effective way to develop conscious control over the diaphragm, whose function is otherwise automatic, albeit less emphatically so, in normal everyday life.

Studying a piece or an entire operatic role also means finely calibrating the expenditure of air in phrases where it is possible to economize without sacrificing the quality of sound, in order to have a sufficient quantity of air available for the more difficult passages (such as a high note following a long phrase).

The amount of air that is consumed depends on how long and demanding the musical phrase is.

In conclusion, the only real possibility of determining the right kind of breath support lies in an analysis of the quality of sound the singer produces. A well-developed, round tone, voice that remains resilient after performance, the ability to sustain extended phrasing over a single breath, the elasticity to handle phrases that call for agility, all these are indications of correct breathing.

These reflections lead us to what should be every singer's fundamental concern: that is, an instinctive urge to improve one's sound, to be able to phrase as one chooses, which means continually searching for the most effective breathing to obtain these results.

Too often young singers blessed with enormous potential may not be sufficiently sensitive to this need and consequently rest on their laurels after only a few years of training without pressing forward in search of the improvement that would allow them to become truly outstanding.

It is also true that some singers begin with good breath support and know how to exploit their vocal emission to best advantage; others must work hard to develop breath support without tension.

All the great singers, however, have either been able to use extremely long breaths or they have learned to breathe more frequently in an "artistic" manner by identifying spots within a musical phrase where an added breath not only is tolerable but may even be an effective expressive device.

THE STUDY OF FOREIGN LANGUAGES

Pavarotti was disadvantaged by the fact that he knew little or no French. This not only attracted cutting remarks from the London critics when he sang *La Fille du Régiment*, it also prevented him from performing some very important operas: *Faust, Carmen, Werther, Les Contes d'Hoffmann*, and forced him to drop Massenet's *Manon* from his repertoire.

The same applies to German, knowledge of which would have allowed him to include *Lohengrin* in his repertoire, not to mention the vast literature of Lieder.

So a young person intending to become a singer should not fail to study at least French and German, the two commonest languages in the operatic and chamber repertoire, together with Russian and of course Italian.

The best way is to find a teacher, preferably a native speaker, who can teach correct pronunciation from the start.

In some languages, however, and particularly in French, some words may need to be pronounced in a special way when set to music. Let's take, for example, the simple phrase "*toute ma vie*". The two final e's are not pronounced in speech, but when sung they must be pronounced if they coincide with a note. So there needs to be some liaison between language teacher and score teacher, in order to establish where the rules of pronunciation must be adapted to fit the music.

It is often forgotten that great composers of the past debated at length about whether or not the French language could be made to fit the requirements of operatic singing.

TECHNICAL APPENDIX No. 8

Chamber Music

Some thoroughly misguided people claim that an opera singer cannot take on the lied or chamber aria repertoire.

Lurking beneath this belief is the idea that the theatrical vocal demands of opera inhibit the more refined expressivity one needs to sing lieder.

Little effort is needed to disprove this thesis. Schwarzkopf, Prey, Fischer-Dieskau, Schreier, Wunderlich, Berganza, Gedda, Gencer, Sciutti, Price, Verret are only a few examples that come to mind from an endless list of excellent opera singers who were equally distinguished interpreters of chamber music.

One would therefore be mistaken to limit oneself exclusively to this particular genre.

The voice should be developed throughout its entire extension, always in search of that power, elasticity, and command of dynamics for which the only complete and exhaustive bench test is the study of opera.

If Pavarotti's experiences are used as a guideline, we may observe how he turned to the chamber repertoire only at the height of his professional career after having all but completely ignored it during his years of study.

Even so, while the chamber aria may not be essential for an exceptionally gifted singer, it is undeniably useful for almost everyone else. It may be seen to function as a link between the simple vocalise and the more complex and elaborate opera aria, an intermediate step that could well be a dangerous one to skip without proper consideration.

In addition, the obvious advantages it offers in terms of interpretation are numerous. Whether learning to recognize stylistic differences among the various composers and to sing in a more intimate manner, with less dramatic force, which can be an effective counter-balance for a certain tendency to exaggerate on the operatic stage; or to be able to convey a situation or a state of mind in just a few bars; or to develop a palette of vocal colors that offer expressive nuance for the sensations, the particular feelings behind the text; all this is immensely helpful and will beneficially stimulate a singer's open-minded interest.

Many teachers believe that students should not perform until they have

reached such a high level of preparation that they are beyond any danger of unpleasant surprises from public or critics.

Apart the fact that not even the greatest artist is impervious to such inconvenience, I maintain that periodically performing for a relatively undemanding audience can actually be extremely useful for the young student.

These occasions are an excellent opportunity for learning how to develop good stage presence and avoid stage fright, not to mention matters of effective voice projection in larger halls; and the public's reception can be a quite useful gauge of one's artistry and vocal skills.

TECHNICAL APPENDIX No. 9

Working with the Conductor

Taking as my point of departure the stormy rapport between Solti and Pavarotti during the preparation of *Otello*, I would like to dedicate this final appendix to an issue that may seem unusual and perhaps has never been addressed in singing manuals: the interaction between the young – or not so young – singer and the conductor.

Let us consider the young singer with his duly earned diploma in hand – or in any case ready to embark upon a career after private study – who decides to apply for auditions in theatres or to participate in voice competitions.

Let us further consider that, after various attempts, he is engaged for the first time and finally sets foot on stage. The individuals who will thereafter evaluate his bravura and with whom he must immediately establish a mutual understanding are two: the stage director and, above all, the conductor.

The influence these two figures may wield is terribly significant and potentially quite insidious as well.

Some directors do not have the slightest concern for the fact that a singer needs to maintain correct posture, forcing him to act on stage in ways that distract his focus from optimum vocal delivery. As for conductors, if a stroke of misfortune should cast the singer into the hands of some pseudo-musician singularly obsessed with rhythmic precision and strict adherence to the concept of song as solfege, then his problems are even greater than those created by the director.

What is one to do? Clearly a novice cannot too strenuously object to the impositions caused by such influential individuals who often exploit the power invested in their respective positions.

Nonetheless, if the singer is able to demonstrate his cultural qualifications with a solid knowledge of opera history and strong musical skills he will be better equipped to defend himself and to solicit dialogue with these potentially dictatorial figures.

It will be necessary to reach an understanding with the conductor regarding the choice of tempi so that they are compatible with your vocal style and interpretation; and beware not to capitulate to demands for an excessive number of rehearsals, which can be a dangerous threat to the health of your voice. If this latter proposition is not possible take care in any case not to sing in full voice – and remember that there are times when a "diplomatic illness" can be a very useful means of staving off such unmitigated threats of vocal assassination.

Many conductors insist on long, sometimes absurdly long breaths. The best thing to do is to comply during rehearsals; then during performance, when the conductor is distracted by orchestral matters, you can preserve your diaphragm from excessive fatigue and concentrate on the most efficient and effective way to use your energy. Obviously with experience you are ever less likely to fall victim to these traps, but it is better to avoid as many of them as possible from the very beginning in order not to risk the fate of so many gifted young singers who have mysteriously disappeared from the scene after only a few short years.

DISCOGRAPHY
The Main Opera Recordings

Vincenzo Bellini

Beatrice di Tenda - London Symphony Orchestra, Richard Bonynge, Joan Sutherland, Luciano Pavarotti (Decca).

I Capuleti e i Montecchi - Orchestra del Teatro alla Scala, Claudio Abbado, Giacomo Aragall, Luciano Pavarotti, Renata Scotto (Opera d'oro).

Norma - Orchestra of the Welsh National Opera, Richard Bonynge, Joan Sutherland, Montserrat Caballé, Luciano Pavarotti, Samuel Ramey (Decca).

I Puritani - London Symphony Orchestra, Richard Bonynge, Joan Sutherland, Luciano Pavarotti, Nicolai Ghiaurov (Decca).

La sonnambula - National Philharmonic Orchestra, Richard Bonynge, Joan Sutherland, Luciano Pavarotti, Nicolai Ghiaurov (Decca).

Arrigo Boito

Mefistofele - National Philharmonic Orchestra, Oliviero De Fabritiis, Nicolai Ghiaurov, Luciano Pavarotti, Mirella Freni, Montserrat Caballé (Decca).

Gaetano Donizetti

L'elisir d'amore - English Chamber Orchestra, Richard Bonynge, Luciano Pavarotti, Joan Sutherland (Decca); Metropolitan Orchestra, James Levine, Luciano Pavarotti, Kathleen Battle, Leo Nucci (Deutsche Grammophon).

La favorita - Orchestra del Teatro Comunale di Bologna, Richard Bonynge, Fiorenza Cossotto, Luciano Pavarotti, Nicolai Ghiaurov (Decca).

La figlia del reggimento - Covent Garden Orchestra, Richard Bonynge, Joan Sutherland, Luciano Pavarotti (Decca).

Lucia di Lammermoor - Covent Garden Orchestra, Richard Bonynge, Joan Sutherland, Luciano Pavarotti, Sherrill Milnes, Nicolai Ghiaurov (Decca).

Maria Stuarda - Orchestra del Teatro Comunale di Bologna, Richard Bonynge, Joan Sutherland, Luciano Pavarotti (Decca).

Umberto Giordano

Andrea Chénier - National Philharmonic Orchestra, Riccardo Chailly, Luciano Pavarotti, Montserrat Caballé, Leo Nucci (Decca).

Ruggiero Leoncavallo

Pagliacci - National Philharmonic Orchestra, Gianandrea Gavazzeni, Julia Varady, Piero Cappuccilli (Decca); Philadelphia Orchestra, Riccardo Muti, Luciano Pavarotti (Philips).

Pietro Mascagni

L'amico Fritz - Covent Garden Orchestra, Gianandrea Gavazzeni, Luciano Pavarotti, Mirella Freni (EMI).

Cavalleria rusticana - National Philharmonic Orchestra, Gianandrea Gavazzeni, Luciano Pavarotti, Julia Varady, Piero Cappuccilli (Decca).

Jules Massenet

Manon - Orchestra del Teatro alla Scala, Peter Maag, Luciano Pavarotti, Mirella Freni, Rolando Panerai (Opera d'oro).

Wolfgang Amadeus Mozart

Idomeneo - Wiener Philharmoniker, Sir John Pritchard, Luciano Pavarotti, Lucia Popp, Agnes Baltsa, Leo Nucci (Decca).

Amilcare Ponchielli

La Gioconda - National Philharmonic Orchestra, Bruno Bartoletti, Luciano Pavarotti, Montserrat Caballé, Agnes Baltsa (Decca).

Giacomo Puccini

La Bohème - Berliner Philharmoniker, Herbert Von Karajan, Mirella Freni, Luciano Pavarotti, Nicolai Ghiaurov (Decca).

Madama Butterfly - Wiener Philharmoniker, Herbert Von Karajan, Mirella Freni, Luciano Pavarotti, Christa Ludwig (Decca).

Manon Lescaut - Metropolitan Orchestra, James Levine, Mirella Freni, Luciano Pavarotti, Cecilia Bartoli (Decca).

Tosca - Orchestra del Teatro dell'Opera di Roma, Daniel Oren, Luciano Pavarotti, Raina Kabaivanska (RCA).

Turandot - London Philharmonic Orchestra, Zubin Mehta, Joan Sutherland, Luciano Pavarotti, Montserrat Caballé, Nicolai Ghiaurov (Decca).

Gioachino Rossini

Guglielmo Tell - National Philharmonic Orchestra, Riccardo Chailly, Luciano Pavarotti, Mirella Freni, Sherrill Milnes, Nicolai Ghiaurov (Decca).

Petite messe solennelle/Stabat Mater - Luciano Pavarotti, Mirella Freni, Lucia Valentini Terrani, Ruggiero Raimondi (Decca).

Richard Strauss

Der Rosenkavalier - Wiener Philharmoniker, Georg Solti, Régine Crespin, Yvonne Minton, Luciano Pavarotti, Helen Donath, Otto Wiener (Decca).

Giuseppe Verdi

Aida - Orchestra del Teatro alla Scala, Lorin Maazel, Maria Chiara, Luciano Pavarotti, Leo Nucci, Ghena Dimitrovna, Paata Burchuladze (Decca).

Don Carlo - Orchestra del Teatro alla Scala, Riccardo Muti, Luciano Pavarotti, Samuel Ramey, Daniela Dessì, Luciana D'Intino (EMI).

Ernani - Orchestra of the Welsh National Opera, Richard Bonynge, Luciano Pavarotti, Joan Sutherland, Leo Nucci, Paata Burchuladze (Decca).

I Lombardi alla prima Crociata - Metropolitan Orchestra, James Levine, Luciano Pavarotti, June Anderson (Decca).

Luisa Miller - National Philharmonic Orchestra, Peter Maag, Montserrat Caballé, Luciano Pavarotti, Sherrill Milnes (Decca).

Macbeth - London Philharmonic Orchestra, Lamberto Gardelli, Dietrich Fischer-Dieskau, Elena Souliotis, Luciano Pavarotti (Decca).

Messa da Requiem - Orchestra del Teatro alla Scala, Riccardo Muti, Cheryl Studer, Luciano Pavarotti, Samuel Ramey (EMI).

Otello - Chicago Symphony Orchestra, Georg Solti, Luciano Pavarotti, Kiri Te Kanawa, Leo Nucci (Decca).

Rigoletto - London Symphony Orchestra, Richard Bonynge, Luciano Pavarotti, Joan Sutherland (Decca); Orchestra del Teatro Comunale di Bologna, Riccardo Chailly, Luciano Pavarotti, June Anderson, Leo Nucci, Nicolai Ghiaurov, Shirley Verrett (Decca); Metropolitan Orchestra, James Levine, Vladimir Chernov, Cheryl Studer, Luciano Pavarotti (Deutsche Grammophon).

La traviata - National Philharmonic Orchestra, Richard Bonynge, Luciano Pavarotti, Joan Sutherland (Decca); Metropolitan Orchestra, James Levine, Luciano Pavarotti, Cheryl Studer (Deutsche Grammophon).

Il trovatore - National Philharmonic Orchestra, Richard Bonynge, Luciano Pavarotti, Joan Sutherland, Marilyn Horne (Decca).

Un ballo in maschera - Orchestra dell'Accademia di Santa Cecilia, Bruno Bartoletti, Renata Tebaldi, Luciano Pavarotti, Helen Donath (Decca); National Philharmonic Orchestra, Georg Solti, Luciano Pavarotti, Margaret Price (Decca).